*To that mischievous wellspring of rollicking mirth known as Katrina Walker, to Cap'n Bob for teaching me to sail, and to the highlander Dr Mairi Macleod for teaching me the things that matter.*
*—Kris Bell*

*For my father, who taught me how to work and the need to care.*
*—Lars Ivar Igesund*

*For Mi Kyoung.*
*—Michael Parker*

# Learn to Tango with D

KRIS MACLEOD BELL, LARS IVAR IGESUND,
SEAN KELLY, AND MICHAEL PARKER

**Learn to Tango with D**

**Copyright © 2007 by Kris Macleod Bell, Lars Ivar Igesund, Sean Kelly, Michael Parker**

ISBN-13 (pbk): 978-1-59059-960-0

ISBN-10 (pbk): 1-59059-960-8

eISBN-13: 978-1-4302-0585-2

Printed and bound in the United States of America (POD)

Trademarked names may appear in this book. Rather than use a trademark symbol with every occurrence of a trademarked name, we use the names only in an editorial fashion and to the benefit of the trademark owner, with no intention of infringement of the trademark.

Java™ and all Java-based marks are trademarks or registered trademarks of Sun Microsystems, Inc., in the United States and other countries. Apress, Inc., is not affiliated with Sun Microsystems, Inc., and this book was written without endorsement from Sun Microsystems, Inc.

Lead Editors: Jason Gilmore and Jeffrey Pepper

Technical Reviewers: Walter Bright and Don Clugston

Editorial Board: Steve Anglin, Ewan Buckingham, Tony Campbell, Gary Cornell, Jonathan Gennick, Jason Gilmore, Kevin Goff, Jonathan Hassell, Matthew Moodie, Joseph Ottinger, Jeffrey Pepper, Ben Renow-Clarke, Dominic Shakeshaft, Matt Wade, Tom Welsh

Project Manager: Beth Christmas

Copy Editor: Marilyn Smith

Associate Production Director: Kari Brooks-Copony

Compositor: Richard Ables

Cover Designer: Kurt Krames

Manufacturing Director: Tom Debolski

Distributed to the book trade worldwide by Springer-Verlag New York, Inc., 233 Spring Street, 6th Floor, New York, NY 10013. Phone 1-800-SPRINGER, fax 201-348-4505, e-mail orders-ny@springer-sbm.com, or visit http://www.springeronline.com.

For information on translations, please contact Apress directly at 2855 Telegraph Avenue, Suite 600, Berkeley, CA 94705. Phone 510-549-5930, fax 510-549-5939, e-mail info@apress.com, or visit http://www.apress.com.

The information in this book is distributed on an "as is" basis, without warranty. Although every precaution has been taken in the preparation of this work, neither the author(s) nor Apress shall have any liability to any person or entity with respect to any loss or damage caused or alleged to be caused directly or indirectly by the information contained in this work.

The source code for this book is available to readers at http://www.apress.com in the Source Code/ Download section.

# Contents

# Foreword

Application developers today can choose from a lot of programming languages, but by and large, most development falls into one of three groups of languages:

- The C and C++ group, where close-to-the-metal, high performance is desired, and the programmer is willing to work hard to get it.

- The Java and C# group, where code is compiled into a "managed" environment. The languages tend to be simpler, and vast libraries of prewritten code are usually available.

- The dynamically typed scripting languages, dominated by Perl, Ruby, and Python. These languages offer rapid development but have poor runtime performance.

Several thousand computer programming languages are in existence, with perhaps a dozen that are in mainstream use. If someone created a new language, who would even look at it? It's not like we had any corporate backing, a marketing department, or a billion dollars to promote it.

So, inspired by the words of Gimli the dwarf, "Certainty of death, small chance of success . . . what are we waiting for?" we set out to invent and establish a new mainstream programming language.

What could have possessed us to do this? While one would think there's a nut for every programming language bolt out there, it turns out that there's a gaping hole. Amazingly, there is no language that enables precise control over execution while offering modern and proven constructs that improve productivity and reduce bugs. What first comes to mind is C++, but C++ remains mired in its need to be backward-compatible with obsolete, decades old decisions. This makes it very difficult for C++ to adopt new ideas. Then there are the languages that compile to virtual machines (VMs) such as Java and C#. But those languages never seem to quite be able to shake off their performance problems, and of course, a VM-based language cannot offer to-the-metal capability.

And lastly, there are the scripting languages such as Perl, Ruby, and Python. These offer many advanced programming features and are highly productive, but have poor runtime performance compared with C++. They also suffer from lingering doubts about their suitability for very large projects.

Often, programming teams will resort to a hybrid approach, where they will mix Python and C++, trying to get the productivity of Python and the performance of C++. The frequency of this approach indicates that there is a large unmet need in the programming language department.

D intends to fill that need. It combines the ability to do low-level manipulation of the machine with the latest technologies in building reliable, maintainable, portable, high-level code. D has moved well ahead of any other language in its abilities to support and integrate multiple paradigms like imperative, OOP, and generic programming.

So why us? How could we possibly succeed with no money, no backing, no paid staff, no marketing department-nothing one would expect to be required for such a monumental task? It turns out that a lot of these apparent disadvantages are actually advantages. The D team doesn't have anyone to answer to (other than the people who use D). We aren't saddled by investors who don't understand what we're doing but want quick monetary results. D doesn't have to fit somewhere in a corporate product line; it isn't positioned as a loss leader to move some other product. There's no marketing department to tell us we have to revamp D to match the latest buzzword *du jour*.

Since we're all volunteers, we are working on D because we genuinely want to and are enthusiastic about D. There aren't any clock-punchers or short-timers working on D.

And lastly, we are free to open source the language.

The D team has other crucial advantages. Many of us have decades of hard-core experience with C, C++, Java, and Perl, and are intimately familiar with what works and what doesn't work. We've worked on one-time throwaway programs and million-line monsters. We've worked on solo teams and professional corporate teams. Many of us are active in the programming community, teaching seminars and giving technology presentations.

D is a labor of love. This book is one of the fruits of that. The authors are all prominent members of the D team. I hope that, reading between the lines, you'll see the joy we take in the elegance with which D expresses the intent of the programmer.

We created D because D is the language we always wanted.

Walter Bright

# About the Authors

**KRIS BELL** is a Scottish pirate and wannabe musician, part-time photographer, avid traveler, open source advocate, miscreant techie dweeb, and a principal Tango contributor. He enjoys swimming, cycling, sailing, and occasional hikes, and recently took up rock climbing. Previously, he dabbled in a bit of car racing and skydiving, and once took a flying-trapeze course (which served only to cement his vocation of choice). He currently lives in California, though he hails from the Scottish west coast and has a dodgy set of bagpipes to remind him of home.

Kris has a varied background in engineering and architecture, spanning application servers to RAD tool sets, embedded operating systems to graphics engines, workflow to high-performance clustering and failover substrata. Some commercial systems he has designed/built include enterprise and Internet application platforms, factory-automation systems, carrier-grade middleware, immersive-environment simulation, and crazy interactive clothing. In a different age, he would probably have been a steam-locomotive engineer, a swashbuckling Jolly Roger, or a funky bell-ringer.

**LARS IVAR IGESUND** holds an MSc in Computer Science from the Norwegian University of Science and Technology, and was involved in the introductory programming course team at the university. Outside the university, he has worked with network administration and support in both public service and private sector, and helped develop 3D graphic systems in C/C++. He is currently selling consultant services through his own company, Igesund Enterprise Software, doing both D and Java projects. Lars Ivar has been involved in the D community since 2003 and has been part of the Tango project lead team since 2006.

**SEAN KELLY** has more than 15 years of experience with C++ and several other programming languages. He is cofounder of the Tango standard library for the open source D programming language. Sean has reviewed articles and books on C++, such as *Imperfect* C++ by Matthew Wilson. A lifelong gamer, he designed and developed a Neverwinter Nights add-on that provides dynamic interserver portaling and event propagation. Sean currently works for Advent Software and lives with his wife and three cats in Concord, California.

**MIKE PARKER**, originally from Atlanta, Georgia, found himself in the Republic of Korea as a U.S. Army medic in the summer of 1991. After volunteering for two more tours in Korea, he left the Army in 1994 to teach English in Seoul. In the intervening years, he has taught English in a variety of environments and has occasionally worked in different capacities for U.S. government contractors in Korea.

In the late 1990s, Mike took up game programming as a hobby. Eventually, his passion for software development expanded beyond games, and he secured a series of Java 2 Platform, Enterprise Edition (J2EE) web application development contracts with several small Korean companies. He discovered D in 2003, and a few months later, created the Derelict project at dsource.org. He became involved with Tango in the fall of 2006.

Currently, Mike is developing his first commercial computer game. He continues to teach English part time in Seoul, Korea, where he lives with his wife Mi Kyoung and their dogs Charlie, Mini, Joey, and Happy.

# About the Technical Reviewer

**DON CLUGSTON** is a physicist who has worked in the solar photovoltaics industry since 1994. An expatriate Australian, he is currently living with his wife and three children in Leipzig, Germany. He has published papers on highly insulated windows, environmental philosophy, Biblical theology, C++ programming, and semiconductor device physics.

After 14 years of experience with C++, Don made his first contributions to D and its standard library in 2005. Since that time, he has had a major influence on the development of the D language, especially with regard to mathematics and generic programming. He is responsible for Tango's mathematics library.

# Acknowledgments

I'd like to thank Don Clugston for his tireless role as technical reviewer, and the community of D enthusiasts across the world who contribute daily to Tango in one way or another-you all know who you are! Also, Tango would not exist without the ongoing efforts of Brad Anderson, who selflessly runs and operates the dsource.org host. Thank you.

Kris Bell

A very big thank you to Inger Merete and Magnus for accepting that I spent vacation time writing parts of this book. Also, thanks to Businesscape for bearing with me during this period, and Jon Espen especially, for valuable input.

Lars Ivar Igesund

I would like to thank my wife Leah for being a constant source of inspiration in my life. Also, thanks to the Tango team, whose expertise and dedication have made Tango a project to be proud of; Don Clugston, for his invaluable insight and criticism; the Tango community, for their unfaltering dedication; and Walter Bright, for creating such a wonderful programming language.

Sean Kelly

Thanks to Walter Bright for creating such a great programming language; to Jason Gilmore for getting the book process going; to Beth Christmas and the other publishing staff we've interacted with, for putting up so patiently with four noob authors; to my coauthors for inviting me to participate in Tango and this book project; and to my wife, Mi Kyoung, for being so understanding and supportive over the past few years while I've spent a tremendously selfish amount of time in front of the computer or with my head buried in books like this one.

Michael Parker

# CHAPTER 1

# First Steps

The D programming language is a strongly typed, natively compiled computer language. If you're familiar with C, C++, or Java, you'll find that you're very much at home with D, as it retains most of the constructs with which many programmers are already comfortable. At the same time, D is different in ways both subtle and striking, successfully combining a number of programming styles while managing to retain a succinct and reasonably simple grammar.

D is designed as a *systems* language, although it is suitable for a wide range of projects, from small programs developed by one person to large-scale, commercial applications worked on by dozens of developers. We were going to tell you all about the advantages of D right here, but Walter Bright stated those so eloquently in the foreword to this book, that we dropped the idea. If you have not yet read the foreword, we highly recommend doing so.

Tango is a general-purpose companion library that provides a rich variety of practical functionality. The Tango library is open source software, with a strong following and an increasingly large number of compatible add-ons available. Tango's design is intended to satisfy a desire for both efficiency and flexibility, mirroring two principal attributes of D itself. The application programming interface (API) offers many services you would expect to find in a modern software development toolkit, such as containers, compression algorithms, threads, fibers, networking, and text manipulation.

This book, *Learn to Tango with D*, is an introduction to both the D language and the Tango library. The key features of both are presented in a condensed and fast-paced format, where the goal is to give you sufficient information to become productive quickly and effectively.

This chapter will give you an overview of the language fundamentals, so bear with us. It demonstrates how to compile and execute programs, and how to install the library and compiler. It also discusses how the language addresses modular development in terms of modules and packages. Subsequent chapters will delve into both language and library specifics. Let's get started!

# Hello World

How about a simple program to output "hello world" to the console? Copy this example into a file called `hello.d` and save it:

```
1.  import tango.io.Stdout;
2.  void main()
3.  {
4.    Stdout ("hello world").newline;
5.  }
```

One of the D language's strengths is that it is familiar to many programmers at a rudimentary level. If you can describe what this example does, you're well on your way to understanding D. Let's take a look at the relevant attributes:

- Line 1 instructs the compiler to enable symbolic access to console output, via the `import` keyword. This operates in a manner roughly equivalent to `#include` in the C++ language or `import` in Java, for those of you familiar with these languages.

- The *entry point* of this example is defined by a `main()` signature on line 2, which the compiler recognizes and treats accordingly. This entry point is considered to be a function, or subroutine, and is invoked during program startup. All functions in the D language must declare a return type. As this example does not actually return a value, line 2 declares the return type to be `void` (effectively, nothing).

- Curly braces {} delimit code blocks and functions in the D programming language, in a manner similar to other languages such as C++ and Java.

- Within the Tango library, `Stdout` represents a generic console-output formatter and serves a similar purpose as `printf()` in C or `System.out.print()` in Java. Line 4 uses `Stdout` exposed via `import` to output the greeting to the console, appending a *newline* for good measure.

- The import of symbols uses dot notation to identify and locate specific functionality within a hierarchy. This example imports `Stdout`, which belongs to the `io` subset of the `tango` library. The hierarchy helps you modularize functionality, and it will be familiar to Java programmers.

- D supports the notion of discrete or modular compilation, demonstrated here through the `import` keyword. We'll discuss this further in the next two sections on modules and packages.

---

Note ➡ Your D compiler may need to be configured in some manner. For now, we assume this has been completed during compiler installation. See the "Installation" section later in this chapter for details.

---

To execute this program, you must compile it, link it with library support, and run it. The first two steps are almost always combined into one step by the compiler itself, which simplifies things. Compilation of D is often managed by a code editor, a dependency program, or an integrated development environment (IDE), but we'll invoke the compiler directly (from the command line) for our examples:

```
dmd hello.d
```

Compilation results in a program called hello.exe on a Windows platform, which you can execute by typing hello on the command line:

```
> hello
```

```
hello world
```

Moving on, it is quite common to pass one or more *arguments* to a command-line program, so let's modify the example to support multiple greetings.

```
1.  import tango.io.Stdout;
2.  void main (char[][] args)
3.  {
4.      if (args.length < 2)
5.          Stdout ("usage is: hello name [name] … [name]").newline;
6.      else
7.          foreach (name; args[1..$])
8.                  Stdout.formatln ("hello {}", name);
9.  }
```

We've introduced a number of additional notions here and are now beginning to show some core features of the language. From the top, this example contains the following:

- Line 2 contains an alternate entry-point signature: main(char[][] args).

- Line 2 uses an array. Command-line arguments are passed to a D program as an array of character arrays, or an array of strings, if you like.

- Arrays expose a number of *properties*. On line 4, we test the length property to see if command-line arguments have been provided. By convention, the first argument provided via main(char[][] args) is the name of the program itself, which we will ignore.

- Array *slicing* allows an array *subset* to be addressed in exactly the same manner as the superset. On line 7, we slice away the first (conventional) command-line argument since it is of no value to us here. Array slices are covered in detail in Chapter 2.

- Line 7 also introduces a foreach mechanism to iterate across a collection. Briefly, foreach exposes elements of the rightmost argument via the left-hand argument(s). This example iterates across a subset of command-line arguments, excluding the element at index zero. The foreach loop is also discussed in Chapter 2.

- Line 8 shows a variation on Stdout that enables formatted output, using {} to indicate positional arguments. The formatting syntax used will be familiar to C# programmers.

Compile and run the modified example with some command-line arguments:

```
> dmd hello.d
> hello Jim Sally
```

```
hello Jim
hello Sally
```

Now let's move on to modular compilation. We'll use the same example to demonstrate how to tease things apart, while retaining a relationship.

# Source Modules

Source files in the D programming language are known as *modules*, and they represent the primary unit of compilation. When you compile a D program, the compiler operates on modules and will generate an object file representing each one. Modules should typically be named with a file extension of .d and identified internally via the module keyword. For example, if we were to split hello.d into two modules, it might take the following form:

```
1.  module greetings;
2.  import tango.io.Stdout;
3.  void hello (char[][] names)
4.  {
5.      foreach (name; names)
6.              Stdout.formatln ("hello {}", name);
7.  }
```

Here, we've migrated console output into a separate module called greetings.d, and identified the module as such on line 1 using the module keyword. On line 3, we've declared a function called hello, which accepts an array of strings and outputs each of them to the console (via lines 5 and 6). Function hello does not return anything at all.

Our main module remains within print.d, although it is modified to look like this:

```
1.  import greetings;
2.  void main(char[][] args)
3.  {
4.      hello (args[1..$]);
5.  }
```

On line 1, we import the greetings module in order to gain access to the contained hello function. Then, on line 4, we pass the same set of arguments to hello as we used in our earlier example. Compilation now requires that both modules be handed to the compiler:

```
> dmd hello.d greetings.d
> hello Jim Sally
```

---

```
hello Jim
hello Sally
```

---

# Package, Import, and Symbol Visibility

As noted in the previous section, a single D source file is known as a D *module*. A collection of related modules within the same directory is known as a *package*. The notion of modules and packages is related to the *visibility* of code, declarations, and identifiers among modules. In other words, packages and modules together determine which symbols can and cannot be seen by other modules in the program (where *symbol* is a generic term for named program elements such as functions, constants, enumerations, structs, classes, and so on).

When you import a module, you're asking for access to the symbols it contains. Where those symbols have been implicitly or explicitly made public, they will be visible to any other importing module. On the other hand, symbols marked as package, private, or protected will *not* be visible to every other module importing them. Here's how these visibility attributes operate, when applied to module symbols:

- public: Any module importing another can access all symbols marked as public.

- package: Only those modules within the same directory, or *package*, can access symbols marked as package.

- protected: Symbols marked as protected are visible only to other modules that derive (subclass) a class encapsulating such attributes

- private: Symbols marked as private are visible only *within* the enclosing module, and are not visible to any outsiders.

To demonstrate, here's a module that exposes various symbols in different ways:

```
1.  module MyModule;
2.  private int x = 10;
3.  package char[] str = "hello";
4.  public void myFunction () {}
5.  public class MyClass {
6.      protected bool yes;
7.  }
```

On line 1, we declare the module name, which must match the file name (without the file extension). Line 2 declares a private integer, which is visible only *within* this specific module. Line 3 declares package visibility for a string, so it can be seen only by modules within the same directory (the same package). Line 4 declares a public function, which is visible to everyone importing this module.

Lines 5 through 7 declare a public class named MyClass, with a protected Boolean attribute. The class itself is visible to any module importing this module, but the protected attribute is visible only to those modules that derive from MyClass.

These visibility attributes are optional, and they are exclusive of one another (it doesn't make sense to combine them). Where visibility is not explicitly indicated, the default for all these cases is public.

Unsurprisingly, import statements themselves have visibility and follow rules similar to those just described for module symbols. A public import of module A into module B will expose the visible symbols of A to module C, where C imports B. Conversely, a private import of module A into module B will *not* expose symbols of A any further. The package and protected declarations operate in a related manner. The one distinction is that the default visibility of import is actually private, in order to help minimize namespace pollution among modules in a nontrivial project. You will learn more advanced ways to use the import statement in Chapter 3.

Throughout the coming chapters, you will see code examples that include something similar to import tango.io.Stdout. In each of these cases, the compiler will expect to locate a module called Stdout.d within a tango/io/ directory, relevant to the -I flag. To make this easier on you, most D compilers will peek into a configuration file, which can dictate what the -I flag (among others) should contain. We'll discuss this configuration file in the next section, which covers compiler installation.

# Installation

In this section, we'll look at installing the compiler and configuring it so that it can locate the files it needs to operate effectively.

At the time of writing, the principal compiler for both Windows and Linux operating systems is the reference compiler named DMD (http://digitalmars.com/d/index.html). Also available is a well-supported front-end for the GNU compiler tools, called GDC (http://dgcc.sourceforge.net/), which emulates the command-line options of DMD. All current D compilers combine both compilation and linking in one step where desired.

D has a very strong online presence, and you can obtain a cutting-edge compiler by visiting the relevant site. However, in the interests of simplifying installation, the most effective approach is to download both the compiler and library as one bundle from the Tango web site (http://www.dsource.org/projects/tango/wiki/Download). The pages there are updated on a regular basis, and the bundled packages cover both the very latest tested combination of compiler and library, along with what is considered to be a solid and stable release.

We're going to install the Windows version of Tango and DMD (the process is similar for the bundled version of the related Linux combination). First, visit the Tango download page at http://www.dsource.org/projects/tango/wiki/DmdDownloads and grab the Windows .zip file. Open the .zip file and expand the content to your disk. For this installation, you should save to a new directory; let's use one called /d. Once the downloaded file is unzipped, examining its content via Windows Explorer or the command line should expose the following list of entries (or similar):

```
Directory of C:\d
          bin
          example
          import
          lib
1,484     LICENSE
  217     README.txt
```

Now set the Windows path to contain /d/bin, so that the compiler and related tools can be located. For example, from the Windows command line, enter the following:

```
> set path=\d\bin
```

After you've set the path, you should be able to enter the command dmd and have the compiler respond.

Now, let's compile and execute an example. Start off by switching to the directory /d/example/console:

```
> cd \d\example\console
```

Next, compile and execute the program there called hello.d:

```
> dmd hello.d
> hello
```

```
hello, sweetheart ☺
```

Congratulations, you've just successfully installed both Tango and D! If you explore a little, you'll find all the Tango source code within /d/import. This is one of the nice things about Tango: all of the source code is readily available.

If you look in /d/bin, you'll find a configuration file, called sc.ini, which is where this particular compiler looks for its default setup and configuration. Open this file with a text editor, and you should see something like the following (abbreviated) content:

```
DFLAGS="-I%@P%\..\import" -version=Tango -L+tango.lib
```

This is where a number of default settings are configured for the DMD compiler you just installed. It includes a -I command pointing at the import directory, a version indicator (-version), and a linker command (-L+) specifying the library tango.lib. You can modify this line as needed, or provide specific flags to the compiler for a particular use case.

---

---

Looking further, you'll also notice a license file and a `readme.txt` file. Please read them both, as they contain important information. Tango is dual-licensed, with an Academic Free License v2.1 and a BSD License. In a nutshell, this means that you can use Tango and D to construct software for your own use or for commercial use without hindrance.

# Compilation Tools

You've seen an example of compiling with more than one source module, but what happens when your project expands to the point where many modules are involved? Several tools are available to assist with this task, such as Make and Ant. The D community felt these could be improved upon in specific ways and has come up with a selection of alternatives, called Jake, Bud, and Rebuild. While you can certainly use traditional automated build tools, it would be worthwhile to consider these alternatives.

Each of the tools is based on a notion that you can compile just a single source module, and the rest of the dependencies will automatically be added to the compilation and linkage task. For example, our earlier `hello.d` example became split into two modules, and thus both needed to be provided to the compiler in order to satisfy the link step. Instead of that approach, we could have used one of these tools, like so:

```
jake hello.d
```

In this scenario, the dependencies within `hello.d` would be added on our behalf, just as though we had explicitly provided them to the compiler. In fact, you can work with the Tango library in this manner if you so choose.

Though Jake, Bud, and Rebuild support a similar strategy, they actually play different roles in the overall process, so choose the one that best suits your task:

*Bud*: This is a full-featured build engine for generating D-based executables, libraries, and dynamic link libraries (DLLs). It has a significant variety of options and was the first tool available. Bud supports Windows and Linux platforms. See `http://dsource.org/projects/build` for more information.

*Rebuild*: This is also a full-featured build tool, with the distinction of being part of a larger source-management, packaging, and installation system called the D Shared Software System (DSSS). It uses the same parser as the compiler itself and runs on a variety of platforms. See `http://dsource.org/projects/dsss` for more information.

*Jake*: This tool is limited to Windows only, and it cannot build libraries. In fact, it doesn't even have any command-line options of its own (you use the same options as the compiler itself). The sole benefit of using Jake is efficiency. It supports extremely fast full compilations, as it causes all modules to be compiled at one time, which can be great with larger projects. Jake is supplied as part of the Tango+D bundle for Windows.

This completes our overview of Tango with D. We've identified some of the key syntax of the D language, introduced a little of the Tango library, and shown how to install Tango and D in a Windows environment. We've also introduced the notion of modules and packages as the mechanism D uses to modularize software development, and how symbols within are exposed through visibility. In the next chapter, we'll dig into the language constructs at a deeper level.

# CHAPTER 2

# D Fundamentals

A movie director once made the observation that Charlie Sheen and Emilio Estevez both resemble their father, Martin Sheen, but look nothing like each other. Something similar might be said of programming languages that belong to the C family. They all share certain features of C, but beyond that, they have several differences. For the most part, the differences are to be found in expanded features, such as inherent support for object-oriented or generic programming, automatic memory management, or features intended to make programs more secure and robust. But at the core of each of these languages is a set of features that vary little from one language to the next. D, too, follows this pattern, but does so in a way that makes it stand out from the rest.

As you'll see in later chapters, some of D's more advanced features improve on ideas already implemented in other modern languages derived from C; some were inspired by languages outside the family; and a few are not to be found in any other mainstream programming language. While these features all contribute to D's unique identity, many users are first drawn to the language by the core feature set. In this chapter, we'll look at these core features.

We'll start out with declarations before moving on to the basic types. Next, we'll look at the different kinds of arrays and array operations. Then we'll get into flow-control constructs. Finally, we'll discuss functions and error handling.

## Declarations

When declaring variables in D, the syntax varies depending on the type of the variable. When we discuss basic types, arrays, and pointers, we'll look at the syntax for variable declarations of each. Before we get that far though, it is helpful to understand some general rules about declarations in D.

# Declaration Syntax and Variable Initialization

D is a *statically typed* language, which means that the type of a variable must be known at
compile time. Therefore, D variable declarations usually require the type to be a part of the
declaration. We say "usually," because there is one exception to this rule, which we'll get to
in a moment. Declarations read from right to left and must be terminated by a semicolon, as
in the following examples:

```
int x;
int y = 1;
char[] myString = "Hello";
float[5] fiveFloats;
long* pointer = null;
```

This code declares one variable x of type int that is not explicitly initialized, and
another variable y of type int that is explicitly initialized to 1. The variable myString is an
example of declaring an initialized, dynamic array. All strings in D are arrays of one of
three character types. fiveFloats is a static array, which is not explicitly initialized in this
example. Finally, the pointer variable is an example of a pointer declaration in D.

Notice that we said that the variables x and fiveFloats are "not explicitly initialized,"
rather than "uninitialized." This is because no D variable is ever left uninitialized at the
point of declaration. If you do not explicitly initialize the variable to some value, it will
automatically be initialized to a specific default value by the compiler. The value used for
initialization depends on the variable's type, but it is guaranteed to be the same for all
variables of the same type. This is a very useful feature for debugging. You'll see the
different default initialization values when we examine each type.

---

Caution ➡ Automatic variable initialization is intended to catch uninitialized variables, a common source of
bugs. However, don't consider it an opportunity to avoid initializing variables yourself. As you'll see when we
discuss floating-point numbers, it is not a good idea get into the habit of relying on automatic variable
initialization to do your job for you.

---

Another important part of a variable declaration is the name, or *identifier*, used to
represent the variable. When creating any identifier—whether it is the name of a variable,
function, class, struct, or whatever—you need to keep a few rules in mind:

- Identifiers can begin with a letter, an underscore (_), or a universal alpha character.

- The first character can be followed by any number of letters or universal alpha characters.

- You can use as many underscores in the identifier as you like, as long as you don't use them for both the first and second characters. Identifiers beginning with two underscores are reserved for use by the compiler.

- Identifiers are case-sensitive, so x and X are not the same.

---

Note ➡ *Universal alphas* are characters from several different languages. They are defined, using hexadecimal codes, in Appendix D of the C99 standard as being legal for use in C identifiers. Because D is derived from C, it accepts the same characters in identifier names.

---

An optional part of variable declaration is the *storage class*. The storage class of a construct determines when it is allocated, where it is stored, how long it lives, how it is accessed, and, in some cases, how the compiler views it. D reserves several keywords for indicating the storage class of different language constructs. In this chapter, we are concerned with only those that affect variables and functions, as using a storage class alters the syntax of a declaration.

A storage class commonly used with individual variables is const. This tells the compiler that a given variable is to be treated as a constant expression, meaning that its value should not change during runtime. Another commonly used storage class is extern, which indicates that a variable is initialized outside the current binary. This is frequently used when creating D modules that interact with C libraries.

When using a storage class in a variable declaration, it must precede the type:

```
const int x = 1;
```

However, in some cases, the type can be omitted:

```
const y = 1;
```

Here, the type of y is omitted. This form uses a feature of D called *automatic type inference*. As long as a declaration contains a storage class, the type can be omitted, and the compiler will infer it automatically. Because a storage class is intended to affect the variable in some way, D provides a special storage class, auto, for those cases where you want to use automatic type inference but don't want any storage class side effects. In other words, auto does not affect the variable in any way at all and indicates only that type inference is to be used. Using auto together with the type in the declaration is not an error, but has no meaning. Here's an example of using the auto storage class:

```
auto x = 1;        // The type will automatically be inferred as int.
auto int y = 1;    // auto has no effect here, since the type is specified.
```

There's quite a bit more to say about declarations. We'll get to the specifics for various constructs as the chapter progresses. First, we need to lay some more groundwork and talk about D's scoping rules.

## Declarations and Scope

The term *scope* describes the context in which a particular declaration resides. Scope affects variable declarations in two ways:

- It determines when and how you can initialize your variables.
- Because scope controls which variables are visible, it also affects how you can name your identifiers.

In this chapter, we are concerned with two basic types of scope: *module scope* and *block scope*. When you create a new D source file, you are working in module scope by default. You usually create a new block scope with each matching pair of curly braces you add to the file.

---

Note ➡ Module scope is also referred to as *global scope*. Block scope is often called *local scope*. D also has a special scope that is unique to classes and structs, generally referred to as class scope. You'll learn about classes and structs in Chapter 3.

---

The following example shows module scope and global scope.

```
// This is module scope. Here, we declare x and initialize it with a constant
// expression.
int x = 1;

void main()
{   // A new block scope starts here--a child of the module scope.
```

```
    // y is declared inside main's block scope, meaning it is local to main.
    // It can see x, but x can't see it.
    int y = x;

    if(1 < 2)
    {   // A new block scope starts here--a child of main's scope.

        // Because x is visible in main's scope, it is also visible here. And
        // because main's scope is this scope's parent, y is visible, too.
        // However, z is visible neither in main's scope nor in the module
        // scope.
        int z = x + y;

    }   // The end of the if block scope

}   // The end of main's block scope

void someFunc()
{   // A new block scope starts here--a child of the module scope and a
    // sibling of main's scope.

    // This y is declared inside someFunc's scope. It can see x, but x can't
    // see it. Also, neither it nor the y in main's scope are visible to each
    // other.
    int y = x;

}   // The end of someFunc's block scope
```

---

Note ➡ The example of using module and block scope employs some features that we haven't yet discussed, such as functions. For now, you just need to focus on the meaning of scope demonstrated by the code. You'll learn about the other features later in this chapter and in upcoming chapters.

---

In this example, the variable x is declared outside any curly braces. This indicates that it is in module scope. The curly braces in the main function introduce a new block scope. It is in this scope that a variable y resides. Similarly, the function someFunc creates a new block scope with its own y variable.

The code comments in the listing explain scope visibility. Essentially, children can see identifiers that are visible in, or declared in, their parent, but parents can never see identifiers declared in their children. Neither can siblings see each other's identifiers.

Bell, et al.

As noted, both `main` and `someFunc` declare a variable y. They can do this since neither scope is visible to the other. However, neither `main` nor `someFunc` could declare a variable x, since x is already visible in both scopes. Identifier names must be unique within the scope in which they are declared. If you create a new identifier using a name that is already visible in that scope, the compiler will fail with an error.

This example also explicitly initializes the variables it declares. Within a block scope, there aren't any restrictions on how you explicitly initialize a variable. However, in the module scope, you can initialize only variables with constant expressions. It is illegal to use a nonconstant expression to explicitly initialize a variable at module scope. Doing so will result in a compiler error. The following shows examples of legal and illegal module scope variable initialization.

```
int x = 1;       // OK: 1 is a constant expression.
int y = x;       // Error: x is not a constant expression.
int z = 1 + 1;   // OK: 1 + 1 is a constant expression.
int a = 1 + x;   // Error: 1 is constant, x is not, so 1 + x is a
                 // nonconstant expression.
```

Because both y and a depend on x, which is a nonconstant expression, neither can be explicitly initialized at module scope. Instead, they should be assigned their values elsewhere in the program in a block scope, such as a function. Assignments, other than those made at the point of declaration, are illegal at module scope. Again, none of these restrictions apply to block scope.

---

Tip ➡ One way to "fake" initialization with nonconstant expressions at the module scope is to make the declaration as normal, without explicitly initializing it, and then assign the variable its value inside a *static module constructor*. A module constructor is a unique D feature that is quite handy for this purpose. You will learn about module constructors in Chapter 4.

---

## CONSTANT AND NONCONSTANT EXPRESSIONS

The term *expression* is often used in language specifications. It is bandied about by compiler writers, who tend to use a great deal of vocabulary that average programmers forgot about after their last comp-sci course, or never knew at all. The D Programming Language specification defines the term as follows (http://www.digitalmars.com/d/expression.html):

*Expressions are used to compute values with a resulting type. These values can then be assigned, tested, or ignored. Expressions can also have side effects.*

Any single value, such a 1 or an x, is an expression. An arithmetic operation, such as 1+1 or 1+x, is an expression. A function call that returns a value is an expression. All of these can be used anywhere the language specification says an expression is legal, such as making an assignment to a variable.

A *constant expression* is one whose value can be known at compile time and is never going to change. For example, 1 is a constant because it is always 1, just as 1+1 always results in the value 2. Because the values of constant expressions never change, the compiler can make certain optimizations with constant expressions that it otherwise wouldn't be able to do.

One popular feature of D is *compile time function execution* (CTFE). This feature is built around constant expressions, allowing programmers to create functions and other expressions that are evaluated at compile time rather than at runtime. This allows the D compiler to make extraordinary optimizations that would not be possible otherwise. You'll learn about CTFE in Chapter 5.

A *nonconstant expression* is one whose value can change, and usually does. For example, the declaration int  x  =  1 assigns a constant expression to the variable x, meaning that the initial value of x is known at compile time, but x itself is nonconstant because it can change at runtime. The compiler is unable to make the optimizations for x that it could make for a constant. This means that x cannot be used where a constant expression is required.

---

For the basic types, which we'll discuss next, the declaration syntax doesn't change from what we've looked at so far. Things do change a bit for pointers, arrays, and functions, as you'll see in the sections about those constructs.

# Basic Types

D supports the same basic types as other languages in the C family, but goes beyond those languages with its own unique twists. For example, D has three character types, nine floating-point types, and a reserved 128-bit integral type that currently doesn't exist in other C languages. All of these are a core part of the language and not specially defined types in a library. In practice, most programmers do not need to be concerned with every data type D supports, but some programmers will put them all to good use. For example, numerical or scientific application programmers will appreciate the variety of floating-point types available.

Something that nearly all of D's basic data types have in common is that the specification explicitly defines the bit size of each. One of the primary benefits of such an approach is that data of a given type will remain the same size across platforms. But there are times when a fixed-size type is not the best option, and you may require a type that is best suited for the current platform. Types with sizes that vary across CPU architectures are available as part of Tango's C modules (which are briefly described in Chapter 8). In fact, the C type size_t is available automatically, without the need to import any additional modules.

In this section, we'll look at integral types, floating-point types, and character types. Most programming books categorize characters as integers. However, characters in D are quite different from other integers and deserve their own section. Before we discuss any of the data types, however, we should first talk about *properties*.

# Properties

All data types in D expose certain properties that can be queried for specific information about the type or, in some cases, can be used to perform a specific operation on a type instance. For example, all types have the sizeof property, which tells the size, in bytes, of a given type. Arrays have a special sort property, which can be used to sort the contents of the array in place. Properties can be queried by using dot notation with the name of the type, as in int.sizeof.

One potentially confusing point about properties is that they can also be accessed through a variable, or instance, of a certain type. If you have a variable x declared as type int, you can query its sizeof property in the same manner: x.sizeof. Keep in mind that, depending on the property, the result you get by querying through the type may not be the same result you get when querying through the variable. Furthermore, some default properties, such as array's sort, work on only type instances and not on the types at all. In the majority of cases, however, the default type properties and instance properties are the same.

Table 2-1 lists properties that are common to all data types and their instances.

*Table 2-1. Properties Common to All Data Types and Their Instances*

| Property | Description |
| --- | --- |
| init | The default initialization value |
| sizeof | The size in bytes |
| alignof | The byte boundary upon which the type or instance is aligned |
| mangleof | A string representing the "mangled" name |
| stringof | A string representing the name of the type or instance as it appears in source code |

Note ➡ When compilers parse source code files, they usually convert the names of functions, variables, and other entities into an internal format that incorporates information about the type or signature of the entity. This form is called the *mangled name*.

The following code queries each of these properties for the type int and for an instance of that type.

```
import tango.io.Stdout;

void main()
{
    Stdout.formatln("int.init is {}", int.init);
    Stdout.formatln("int.sizeof is {}", int.sizeof);
    Stdout.formatln("int.alignof is {}", int.alignof);
    Stdout.formatln("int.mangleof is '{}'", int.mangleof);
    Stdout.formatln("int.stringof is '{}'", int.stringof);

    int x;
    Stdout.formatln("x.init is {}", x.init);
    Stdout.formatln("x.sizeof is {}", x.sizeof);
    Stdout.formatln("x.alignof is {}", x.alignof);
    Stdout.formatln("x.mangleof is '{}'", x.mangleof);
    Stdout.formatln("x.stringof is '{}'", x.stringof);
}
```

The result of compiling and executing this code is as follows:

```
int.init is 0
int.sizeof is 4
int.alignof is 4
int.mangleof is 'i'
int.stringof is 'int'
x.init is 0
x.sizeof is 4
x.alignof is 4
x.mangleof is 'i'
x.stringof is 'x'
```

As you can see from this example, the only property that shows different results for the type and instance queries is stringof, which is inherently different from instance to instance due to what it represents. You may encounter other properties that differ between a type and an instance. So before you use a particular property, make sure you understand what it represents so that you can make the appropriate query.

## Integral Types

*Integral types* are types that represent integer values. Nearly all integral types in D come in two flavors:

- *Signed types* can represent both positive and negative numbers.
- *Unsigned types* can represent only positive numbers. They have the same name as the corresponding signed type, but with a u prefix.

Table 2-2 shows each integral type, its size in both bits and bytes, and the minimum and maximum values it can represent.

*Table 2-2. Integral Types*

| Type | Size (Bits) | Size (Bytes) | Min | Max |
| --- | --- | --- | --- | --- |
| byte | 8 | 1 | −128 | 127 |
| ubyte | 8 | 1 | 0 | 255 |
| short | 16 | 2 | −32768 | 32767 |
| ushort | 16 | 2 | 0 | 65535 |
| int | 32 | 4 | −2147483648 | 2147483647 |
| uint | 32 | 4 | 0 | 4294967295 |
| long | 64 | 8 | −9223372036854775808 | 9223372936854775807 |
| ulong | 64 | 8 | 0 | 18446744073709551615 |

The bool data type is not listed in Table 2-2 because it has only two possible values and is neither signed nor unsigned. A bool is 1 byte in size and can be either true or false. It can be converted to any integral type, at which time `true` will be converted to `1` and `false` to `0`. The default value of a `bool` is `false`.

Also missing from Table 2-2 are `cent` and `ucent`, both of which are intended to be 128 bits, or 16 bytes, in size. Currently, neither is implemented. However, the keywords `cent` and `ucent` are reserved for future use.

With the exception of `long` and `ulong`, the default initialization value of all integral types is `0`. In a perfect world, the default would be an invalid value. Unfortunately, in all of the range of values that an integral type can hold, none of them are inherently invalid. So, we have to settle for `0`.

In D, all constant integer values are of type `int`. D supports a special modifier, `L`, that can be appended to an integer constant to make it type `long` instead of `int`. The initialization value of both `long` and `ulong` is `0L`.

---

Note ➡ The distinction may seem minor, but internally there is a big difference between `0` and `0L`. The former is a 32-bit value and is treated as an `int`, whereas the latter is a 64-bit value and is treated as a `long`. Appending `L` to any constant values you assign to `long` variables is a good habit.

---

In addition to the properties listed in Table 2-1, integral types expose the two properties shown in Table 2-3. The values these properties return are listed in the Min and Max columns of Table 2-2.

*Table 2-3. Properties Specific to Integral Types*

| Property | Description |
| --- | --- |
| `min` | Minimum value this type can represent |
| `max` | Maximum value this type can represent |

## Floating-Point Types

In layman's terms, a *floating-point* type is any type whose values contain a decimal point. In most programming languages, the built-in floating-point types are used to represent what mathematicians call a *real number*. A real number is one that includes the numbers between the integers. For example, the number 1.011 can represent a real number in mathematical terms and is a floating-point value in programming terms.

Although D supports nine floating-point types, the average user of D will probably be interested in only two of the three basic floating-point types: float and double. These two types, and one more called real, represent real numbers in the mathematical sense. But D goes beyond built-in support for real numbers. It offers three floating-point types that represent *imaginary numbers* and three more that represent *complex numbers*. If you don't know the difference between real, imaginary, and complex numbers, you'll likely have no use for these other types.

After reading about the integral types in the previous section, you might think that the default initializer for floating-point types is 0.0. Many newcomers to D incorrectly make that assumption. The default initializer for floating-point types is actually a form of a special value called Not a Number (NaN), which helps to detect errors caused by uninitialized variables. Each floating-point type has a nan property, which is used to initialize it. Outside initialization, if you find yourself with a floating-point value equivalent to NaN after a calculation, you can be fairly certain that you have a programming error.

Table 2-4 lists all of D's floating-point types, their size in bits and bytes, and the default initializer as defined in the language specification.

*Table 2-4. Floating-Point Types*

| Type | Size (Bits) | Size (Bytes) | Initializer |
|------|-------------|--------------|-------------|
| float | 32 | 4 | float.nan |
| double | 64 | 8 | double.nan |
| real | Platform dependent | Platform dependent | real.nan |
| ifloat | 32 | 4 | float.nan * 1.0i |
| idouble | 32 | 8 | double.nan * 1.0i |
| ireal | Platform dependent | Platform dependent | real.nan * 1.0i |
| cfloat | 64 | 8 | float.nan * float.nan * 1.0i |
| cdouble | 128 | 16 | double.nan * double.nan * 1.0i |
| creal | Platform dependent | Platform dependent | real.nan * real.nan * 1.0i |

The types float and double are the standard fare found in any C-family programming language. The real type is defined to be the largest size on the hardware used to compile the application. For example, on x86 platforms, a `real` is 80 bits (10 bytes) in size. The types prefixed with an `i` represent imaginary numbers. The types prefixed with a `c` represent complex numbers.

   In addition to the properties listed Table 2-1, floating-point types expose all of the properties shown in Table 2-5. The average programmer will likely be concerned with only the `nan`, `max`, and `min` properties.

*Table 2-5. Properties Specific to Floating-Point Types*

| Property | Description |
| --- | --- |
| infinity | Value that is too large to represent |
| nan | Value used to represent NAN |
| dig | Number of decimal digits of precision |
| epsilon | Smallest increment to the value 1 |
| mant_dig | Number of bits in the mantissa |
| max_10_exp | Maximum power of 10 exponent this type can represent |
| max_exp | Maximum power of 2 exponent this type can represent |
| min_10_exp | Minimum power of 10 exponent this type can represent as a normalized value |
| min_exp | Minimum power of 2 exponent this type can represent as a normalized value |
| max | Largest value this type can represent that is not infinity |
| min | Smallest normalized value this type can represent that is not 0 |
| re | Real part of the number |
| im | Imaginary part of the number |

---

Tip ➡ If you find some of the terminology used in this section puzzling, you might want to visit the Wikipedia page about floating-point numbers (http://en.wikipedia.org/wiki/Floating_point). There, you can learn what a mantissa is, what normalization means, and a great deal more. At the very least, it should give you a better understanding of what some of the floating-point properties represent.

---

Another important thing to mention here is that the `re` and `im` properties are instance properties, rather than type properties. If you try to access either of them through a type, such as `float.re`, you will be confronted with a compiler error. This is because, by definition, both properties require a number to exist. There's no such thing as the real or imaginary part of the type `float`, but these parts do exist in the number `1.11`. So assuming that you have a variable of type `float` named `f`, you can access both properties through it: `f.im`.

You can read more about D's floating-point types, including the rationale behind including complex and imaginary types in the language, at http://www.digitalmars.com/d/1.0/float.html.

## Character Types

Whereas most languages in the C family support only one character type, D supports three. What makes D's character types different from integrals is that they don't necessarily represent integer values. More accurately, each type is intended to represent a Unicode code point. Several different Unicode encodings exist. D's character types provide built-in support for the three most common encodings.

Another big difference between integrals and characters is the default initializer. Remember that the goal of automatic initialization is to aid in debugging. Ideally, all built-in data types would be initialized to an invalid value. Integrals do not have invalid values. Floating-point values do. Since D's character types represent Unicode code points, they also have values that are invalid. Specifically, certain values are not valid Unicode. D uses three such values as the default initializer for each character type.

Table 2-6 lists each character type, its size in both bits and bytes, the Unicode encoding it represents, its minimum and maximum values, and it default initializer.

*Table 2-6. Character Types*

| Type | Size (Bits) | Size (Bytes) | Unicode Encoding | Min | Max | Initializer |
|------|-------------|--------------|------------------|-----|-----|-------------|
| char | 8 | 1 | UTF-8 | 0 | 255 | 0xFF |
| wchar | 16 | 2 | UTF-16 | 0 | 65535 | 0xFFFF |
| dchar | 32 | 4 | UTF-32 | 0 | 1114111 | 0x0000FFFF |

Individual characters can be used anywhere an integral can. Each character type also exposes the same properties that integrals do, as listed in Table 2-3.

When we look at strings later in this chapter (in the "Strings" section), you'll see that they are sequences of characters. D programmers generally work with strings more frequently than with individual characters, but character types come in handy when you're modifying strings or searching them to find a specific character. Character values can be assigned any integer value that is valid for an integral of the same bit size, such as char c = 10, or can be assigned a single-quoted letter, such as char c = 'a'.

That wraps up the three basic data types. Now it's time to take a quick look at pointers, and then move on to arrays.

# Pointers

In short, a *pointer* is a variable that represents a memory address rather than actual program data. Often, the address "points" to program data, such as the beginning of a series of integers or other data type. We mention pointers here because those with experience in C or C++ need to know that pointers work a bit differently in the world of D.

First, pointer declarations are subtly different in D than in C. Consider the following line of code:

```
int *x, y;
```

This code is valid in both the C and D languages, but has different results in each. In C, x is a pointer to int, and y is an int, not a pointer. In D, both x and y are pointers to int. This is a subtle, but very important, distinction.

When you use D's typeof operator on an int, the type returned is int. But use the typeof operator on a pointer to int, and the type returned is int*. Because of this, it is more common for D programmers to move the asterisk over to the left, transforming the preceding declaration into the following:

```
int* x, y;
```

By using this syntax, it is clear that you are declaring two int pointers. It is good practice to follow this convention for all pointer declarations.

Another thing to know about D pointers is that there is no -> operator. Struct and class pointers are manipulated using dot notation. However, you can still use the syntax *x to dereference the pointer.

---

Note ➡ If you have no idea what pointers are, a good place to start learning about them and some of the terminology used in this section is the Wikipedia page about pointers (http://en.wikipedia.org/wiki/Pointer). Not only does this page discuss pointers in general terms, but it also gives a little background about pointer usage in different languages.

---

Finally, because D has built-in garbage collection, you need to adhere to a few restrictions when using pointers that point to garbage-collected memory. Most of these restrictions relate to a number of pointer tricks that C programmers have implemented over the years, such as using the low-order bits of a pointer to store extra data. In a nutshell, don't do anything that depends on the address of the pointer to stay the same. Pointers that point to memory not managed by the garbage collector are free from these restrictions. For details, see http://www.digitalmars.com/d/1.0/garbage.html.

# Arrays

An *array* is a sequence of data, usually of the same type, that can vary in length and is stored in a contiguous block of memory. D supports four types of arrays as part of the core language: *static arrays*, *dynamic arrays*, *strings*, and *associative arrays*. We'll look at each in turn. We'll also discuss array operations. But first, let's examine some things that all arrays have in common.

Conceptually, you can think of a D array as an item that is made up of two components: a pointer and a length. The pointer points to the memory address that contains the first element in the array, and the length represents the number of elements in the array. Both the length and the pointer are accessible as properties. Because each array knows how many elements it contains, it is possible for the compiler to do automatic bounds checking (DMD does this by default, but it can be turned off by passing -release on the command line).

D supports the same syntax as C for array declarations, called *postfix syntax*, but only for backward compatibility.

```
// C-style, or postfix, declarations
int x[3];         // Declares an array of 3 ints
int x[3][5];      // Declares 3 arrays of 5 ints
int (*x[5])[3];   // Declares an array of 5 pointers to arrays of 3 ints
```

The preferred syntax is called *prefix* syntax.

```
// D-style, or prefix, declarations
int[3] x;         // Declares an array of 3 ints
int[3][5] x;      // Declares 5 arrays of 3 ints
int[3]*[5] x;     // Declares 5 pointers to arrays of 3 ints
```

The syntactical differences between the two styles are obvious, but prefix multidimensional array declarations can be confusing to those with a C background. You'll notice that the order is reversed from the postfix declarations. However, indexing values from the multidimensional arrays is done in the same way, no matter how they are declared, as in the following example.

```
int x[5][3];      // Postfix declaration of 5 arrays of 3 ints
int[3][5] y;      // Prefix declaration of 5 arrays of 3 ints

x[0][2] = 1;      // The third element of the first array is set to 1.
y[0][2] = 2;      // the third element of the first array is set to 2.
```

As you can see, postfix and prefix come into play only in array declarations. You index them both in the same way.

## Static Arrays

Static arrays are the simplest to understand; in fact, all of the arrays declared in the previous examples are static. These are arrays that have a fixed length that is established at compile time. The length of a static array can never change during the course of program execution. Static arrays are allocated on the stack. Table 2-7 lists the properties that are unique to static arrays (remember that these are in addition to the properties listed in Table 2-1, which are common to all data types).

*Table 2-7. Properties Specific to Static Arrays*

| Property | Description |
| --- | --- |
| length | Number of elements in the array; cannot be modified |
| ptr | Pointer to the first element in the array |
| dup | Creates and returns a dynamic array that is an exact duplicate of the array |
| reverse | Reverses the array in place and returns the array |
| sort | Sorts the array in place and returns the array |

Unlike most of the properties that you have seen so far, each of those listed in Table 2-7 is exclusively an instance property, and three of the static array properties have side effects. The dup property will allocate enough memory to hold an exact duplicate of the array. The reverse and sort properties will change the order of items in the array. While these are very convenient properties to use, be aware that they could have performance implications when used on large arrays or in performance-critical code.

Note ➡ The sizeof property of a static array (see Table 2-1) returns the length of the array multiplied by the number of bytes per array element. This means that the result varies based on the type and number of elements in the array.

# Dynamic Arrays

Unlike with static arrays, the length of a dynamic array does not need to be known at compile time. Dynamic arrays are allocated on the heap. Because the length is not fixed, a dynamic array can be resized as needed. Up to now, all of the properties you have seen have been read-only. The length property of dynamic arrays is actually writable. To resize the array, simply set its length property to the new size.

You make an array dynamic by declaring it without any numbers to indicate the size of the array. Instead, you use empty brackets, as follows:

```
int x[];   // Postfix dynamic array declaration
int[] y;   // Prefix dynamic array declaration
```

Neither of the arrays in this example allocates any space for its elements. Both arrays are empty, meaning each has a length of 0 and a null pointer.

You can allocate space for a dynamic array in three ways:

- Use D's new keyword.

- Explicitly set the length property to the number of elements required.

- Use an array literal. An *array literal* is a sequence of values contained within brackets, such as [0,2,5,6] or [2.0, 5.0, 3.0].

The following shows examples of these methods.

```
int[] x = new int[10];      // A dynamic array of 10 ints all initialized to int.init
int[] y;                    // An empty dynamic array of ints
y.length = 10;              // y can now hold 10 ints.
int[] z = [0,1,2,3,4];      // A dynamic array that holds 5 ints initialized to
                            // the values 0, 1, 2, 3, and 4
int[5] z1 = [0,1,2,3,4];    // A static array of 5 ints initialized to the values
                            // 0, 1, 2, 3, and 4
int[] a;                    // An empty dynamic array
a= new int[10];             // a can now hold 10 ints. All values are now set
                            // to int.init
a.length = 5;               // a has been resized to hold only 5 ints.
a = [0,1,2,3,4,5];          // a now has a length of 6 and contains the values
                            // 0, 1, 2, 3, 4, and 5
```

No matter how the space for a dynamic array is initially allocated, whether via new or its length property, it can be resized at any time. Typically, you resize an array by adjusting its length property, by appending new values to the array, by copying one array to another, or by assigning an array literal to the reference. If the new length is greater than the old length, more space is allocated to accommodate it. If the new length is less than the old length, no memory operations are performed, meaning nothing is allocated, reallocated, or freed.

In addition to the properties listed in Table 2-1, dynamic arrays expose all of the properties that static arrays do, as listed in Table 2-7. The only difference is that the length property of a dynamic array is not constant, so it is both readable and writable.

---

Note ➡ The sizeof property of a dynamic array (see Table 2-1) returns the size, in bytes, of the array reference rather than the amount of memory used by the array.

---

# Strings

In D, strings are not so much a separate array type as they are a special case of normal static and dynamic arrays. Strings are arrays that are of type char, wchar, or dchar and represent UTF-8, UTF-16, and UTF-32 sequences, respectively.

String literals can be used to initialize a new string. A *string literal*, frequently just referred to as a *string*, is a sequence of characters contained within double quotation marks, such as "Hello World". Strings initialized with a string literal are immutable, meaning they cannot be modified. Because strings are arrays, they can be static or dynamic.

Here are examples of initializing strings:

```
char[] s1 = "abcd";  // s1 is a dynamic array.
s1[0] = 'x';         // since s1 is immutable, this should be an error. Although
                     // the compiler does not complain, this could cause a crash.
char[4] s2 = "abcd"; // s2 is a static array.
s2[0] = 'x';         // Again, this could cause a crash since s2 was initialized
                     // with a string literal.
```

Another special feature of strings is that a postfix can be attached to a string literal in order to specify how it should be treated by the compiler. By default, the type of a string is determined automatically during compilation. However, you can use the postfix character c, w, or d to force a literal to be treated as an array of char, wchar, or dchar, respectively. For example, the literal "hello"w will be treated as an array of wchar because of the w postfix.

Tango provides several library functions that operate on strings. These include functions to convert between one string type and another. While it is possible to cast between string types, such as from wchar[] to dchar[] and vice versa, this is a technique that should be used cautiously. Because each character type represents a different Unicode encoding, it is possible that casting from one type to the other could have unexpected results. A safer approach is to use Tango's Unicode conversion routines instead. You'll learn about Tango's text-processing functions in Chapter 6.

There are no special properties exposed by strings, other than those exposed by static and dynamic arrays. Which properties are available depends on how the string was allocated.

# Associative Arrays

Associative arrays are distinct from static and dynamic arrays. What sets them apart is that they are allowed to be indexed by types other than integers and they can be sparsely populated. Associative arrays must be declared to hold values of a certain type and to have keys of a certain type. D's associative arrays are analogous to hash maps in other languages. They are dynamic by nature and always reside on the heap. The following example shows some different associative array declarations.

```
int[char[]] x;      // An associative array with values of type int and keys of type
                    // char[]
float[double] y;    // An associative array with values of type float and keys of
type
                    // double
char[][char[]] z;   // An associative array with values of type char[] and keys of
                    // type char[]
```

Once an associative array has been declared, you can associate values with keys using the following syntax:

```
aa[key] = value;
```

If any value is already associated with the given key, it will be overwritten. You can retrieve values from an associative arrays using similar syntax:

```
value = aa[key];
```

If a key does not exist in the associative array, the D runtime will throw an error indicating that the array index is out of bounds. One way to avoid this is to test if the key exists using the in operator, which we'll look at shortly.

Associative arrays have a few unique properties, which are listed in Table 2-8.

*Table 2-8. Properties Specific to Associative Arrays*

| Property | Description |
| --- | --- |
| length | Number of values in the associative array; as with static arrays, this is read-only |
| keys | Dynamic array containing all of the keys in the associative array |
| values | Dynamic array containing all of the values in the associative array |
| rehash | Reorganizes the associative array in place to make lookups more efficient and returns the new array |

Because of the nature of an associative array, it doesn't make sense to be able to modify the number of key/value pairs it contains without adding and removing them, so the length property is read-only. The rehash property is an expensive operation, but can result in more efficient lookups if a large number of keys have been set.

---

Note ➡ The sizeof property of an associative array (see Table 2-1) returns the size, in bytes, of the array reference, rather than the amount of memory used by the array.

---

In the next section, we'll look at some operations that can be performed on dynamic and static arrays. Since associative arrays have their own unique set of operations, we'll cover two handy associative array operators here:

in: This operator can be used to determine if a value has been associated with a given key in an associative array. This is very handy to avoid overwriting a key that already exists, for example. The in operator returns a pointer to the value if it exists and null if it doesn't.

remove: This function is called through an associative array much like a property, but you pass a key value as an argument (you'll learn more about functions later in this chapter, in the "Functions" section). When the remove function is called, it removes the key and its associated value from the array.

Here is an example that uses both in and remove:

```
int[char[]] aa;      // Declare an associative array of int values and char[] keys.
aa["One"] = 1;       // Associate the value 1 with the key "One".
int x = aa["One"];   // Retrieve the value associated with the key "One".
int *y = ("Two" in aa);     // See if the key "Two" has been set.
if(y is null)
{
    aa["Two"] = 2;          // Only set "Two" if it isn't set already.
}
aa.remove("One");    // Remove the key "One" and its associated value.
```

## Array Operations

Both static and dynamic arrays (and, as such, strings) have certain operations that can be performed using different operators. For example, as you have already seen, the [] operator is used in declarations, as well as to set and get array values. It is also used in slicing and copying, which we will look at now, before moving on to concatenation.

## Slicing

*Slicing* is an operation that essentially creates another view of an array. It does not copy any array data, but simply creates a new array reference that shares a portion of an existing array. In other words, it's a different view of the same data.

A slice is performed using the following syntax:

```
a[start .. end]
```

where start is the index at which the slice begins, and end is one index beyond the index where the slice should end.

If you are slicing an entire array, you can use the shorthand [ ], without specifying the start and end points, thereby creating an identical view of the existing array.

Here are examples of slicing:

```
int x[] = [0, 1, 2, 3, 4];
int y[] = x[1 .. x.length];    // y is a view of x starting from the second index
                               // and ending with the last, i.e., 1, 2, 3, 4.
int z[];
z = x[1 .. x.length -1];       // z is a view of x starting from the second index
                               // and ending with the next-to-last, i.e., 1, 2, 3.
int all = x[];                 // all is a view of all of x, from the first
                               // element to the last, i.e., 0, 1, 2, 3, 4.
```

In the next chapter, you'll see how to implement custom slicing operations on your own data types using operator overloading.

---

Tip ➡ In a slice operation, when you use the length of the array you are slicing as one of the end points, you can substitute the call to the length property with the special $ operator. For example, x[1 .. x.length] can be rewritten as x[1 .. $].

---

## Copying

In D, you can copy an array in three ways:

- Manually fetch the values from an array and assign them all to another array of the same length. This is rather inefficient and should never be the first choice.

- Use the dup property common to all static and dynamic arrays.

- Use the slice operator ([ ]).

In the previous section, you learned that an array slice does not copy an array, but instead creates a new reference that shares part of the same data. However, you can use the slice operator in a copying operation by placing it on the left side of an assignment and another array on the right side. The following example demonstrates how to copy arrays using the slice operator.

```
int[] x = [0, 1, 2, 3, 4];
int[] y = x;                // All 5 elements of x are copied to y.
int[] z = x[];              // All 5 elements of x are copied to z.
y[0 .. 2] = x[1 .. 3];      // Same as y[1] = x[2];.
```

Although the example uses only dynamic arrays, the same operations can be performed using static arrays.

## Concatenation

D has a special binary operator, ~, which is used to perform array concatenation. This operator works with any array, but it is most often used with strings. You can also use the ~= operator, which effectively appends one array to another in place. Here are some examples of array concatenation:

```
char[] x = "Hello";
char[] y = "World";
char[] z = x ~ " " ~ y;     // z is a new string, "Hello World", while x an y are
                            // unchanged.

int[] a = [0, 1, 2, 3];
int[] b = [4, 5];
a ~= b;                     // a now contains the values 0, 1, 2, 3, 4, and 5, while
                            // b is unchanged.
```

As with the slice operator, custom concatenation behavior can be implemented using operator overloading, as described in the next chapter.

# Flow Control

In computer programming, *flow control* refers to language constructs that direct the flow of program execution. D supports three basic types of flow-control constructs: conditionals, loops, and goto.

## Conditionals

A *conditional* is a construct that branches based on a true or false condition. D supports three different types of conditionals: if-else blocks, the ternary operator, and switch-case constructs. All of these can be found in other C-family programming languages, with very few differences.

### if-else Blocks

Perhaps the most commonly used conditional is the form often referred to as an if-else block. These conditionals always begin with an if statement that tests for a certain condition and will execute only if that condition evaluates to true. This statement can be followed by any number of else if statements, which test for more conditions that will execute only if they evaluate to true. Optionally, a final else statement can execute if none of the preceding conditions evaluated to true. The following are examples of if-else blocks.

```
bool x = true;
if(x)
{
    // This will execute because x is true.
}
else
{
    // This will not execute because x is true.
}

bool y = false;
int a = 1;
int b = 2;
```

```
if(y)
{
    // This will not execute because y is false.
}
else if(a > b)
{
    // This will not execute because a > b evaluates to false.
}
else
{
    // This will execute because both of the two preceding conditions evaluated
    // to false.
}
```

if-else blocks can be nested inside each other for as many levels as you have stack space available. Realistically, nested if-else blocks are quite ugly and hard to follow, so most programmers rarely go beyond two or three levels deep. If you find yourself going deeper, you probably need to rethink your design.

## The Ternary Operator

Often, you don't need to perform any overly complicated action based on an if-else conditional. For example, you might need to simply assign a value to a single variable based on a specific condition. This is where the *ternary operator* comes in handy. If you need to perform more than one operation for each statement, however, you should stick with the if-else block.

The ternary operator consists of two characters: ? and :. The entire expression takes the following form:

```
condition ? true action : false action
```

where true action and false action are expressions that will be evaluated if condition is true or false, respectively.

The following example shows how you can replace a single assignment in an if-else block with the ternary operator.

```
int x;
int y = 1;
int z = 2;

// The if-else block
if(y < z)
{
```

```
    x = 1;
}
else
{
    x = 0;
}
```

```
// The same code using a ternary operator
```

```
x = y < z ? 1 : 0;
```

The ternary operator should be used sparingly, because overuse can make code confusing and ugly.

---

Caution ➡ When using a ternary operator to assign a value to an `auto` variable, the result may not be what you expect. Variables declared `auto` will take the type of the last item in the ternary expression, regardless of the type actually assigned. So if the expression `auto a = b ? c : d` evaluates to c, the type of a will become the type of d. If c and d are the same type, this doesn't matter, but it is something to be aware of when using multiple types in a ternary expression.

---

## switch-case Statements

`switch-case` is another conditional construct that is often considered to be an ideal alternative to `if-else` blocks when you have several conditions to test or when you need to test for specific values rather than Boolean conditions.

You start with a `switch` statement that evaluates an expression. The `switch` statement creates a new scope in which you implement several `case` statements that evaluate expressions that correspond to the possible values the `switch` evaluated. You may also end the `switch` with a special `default` statement, which does not evaluate an expression and executes only if no `case` matched the result.

You need to keep in mind a few restrictions on both `switch` and `case` statements:

- The expression evaluated by the `switch` must result in an integral type, including character types, or a string.

- The expressions in each `case` statement must evaluate to a constant value or array.

- The resultant value in each `case` statement must be implicitly convertible to the type of the evaluated result in the `switch`.

- Each value in the case statements must be unique. It is illegal to have two case statements whose expressions evaluate to the same value.

The following shows the switch-case statement in action.

```
int x = 1;
int y;
int z;
switch(x)
{
    case 2 - 1:    // Evaluates to case 1:
        y = 2;
        break;
    case 1 + 1:    // Evaluates to case 2:
        y = 3;
        break;
    case 3:
        y = 5;
    case 4:
        z = 2;
        break;
    default:
        break;
}
```

Notice the break statements here. break is a statement that can be used in a switch or a loop as a quick exit. The case statements containing the break statements will cause the switch to exit as soon as they execute the code before the break. For example, in the first case, after y = 2 executes, the switch will exit. Notice, however, that the third case has no break statement. This means that after y = 5 is evaluated, execution will "fall through" to the next case, so that z = 2 is executed. Essentially, every case without a break statement will fall through to the next until a break is encountered.

Much of what you have seen here is the same in D as it is in other C-family languages. However, one thing that D does differently is to accept strings in both the switch and case statements. For example, the following is possible in D:

```
char[] str;
switch(str)
{
    case "Hello":
        . . .
    case "World":
        . . .
```

```
        . . .
}
```

You can always use library functions to compare different strings, but the ability to use strings in `switch-case` blocks can greatly simplify code.

# Looping Constructs

A *loop* is a block of code that executes repeatedly until a certain condition is met. D supports five different loops, but for our purposes, we will split them up into three categories: `for`, `while`, and `foreach`.

In loops, the `break` and `continue` statements provide a way to exit. You've already seen `break` in the discussion of `switch-case` constructs. In loops, it serves the same function: an early exit. If you are performing an operation in a loop and determine that you no longer need to repeat the operation, you can execute a `break` statement and exit the loop immediately, rather than waiting for it to run its course. This is often used as an optimization in loops that are searching a data structure for a specific value, because once the value is found, you don't need to continue searching.

The `continue` statement is also handy. Rather than exiting the entire loop as `break` does, it exits the current iteration and continues to the next. The effect is that any code following the `continue` statement will not be executed in the same iteration in which `continue` is called. This statement is usually wrapped in a conditional, as it would be rather silly to call it on every iteration. The result is that the code following a `continue` will execute on some iterations, and it won't execute on other iterations.

## for Loops

The venerable `for` loop has found a place in many different programming languages, both inside and outside the C family. D's version follows the traditional form. The loop declaration consists of three expressions that are evaluated at different points.

The form of the declaration is as follows:

```
for(initializer; termination condition; per-iteration action) { }
```

where:

- The `initializer` expression is evaluated only once when the loop is getting ready to start.

- The `termination condition` is evaluated at the beginning of each iteration (and on the first iteration, just after the initializer).

- The `per-iteration action` is evaluated at the end of each iteration.

These can each actually be *expression lists* (multiple, comma-separated expressions), and each expression in the list will be evaluated in the order it appears.

Here's an example of using a `for` loop.

```
for(int i=0; i < 100; ++i)
{
    // Do something you want to repeat 100 times.
}
```

At the start of this loop, the variable `i` is initialized to 0. Because it is part of the loop declaration, `i` is part of the loop's scope and is not visible outside it. At the beginning of each iteration, the loop checks the termination condition and will quit if `i` is no longer less than 100. At the end of each iteration, `i` is incremented by 1. The result is that the loop will execute 100 times before terminating.

## while Loops

D supports two forms of `while` loops: the standard `while` and the special `do..while`, also called the do loop.

Unlike the `for` loop, a `while` loop has only one expression to evaluate: a termination condition, which is evaluated at the beginning of each iteration. If any variables need to be updated, that must be done within the loop. The `while` syntax is as follows:

```
while(termination condition) { }
```

The do loop is very similar to the `while` loop. It also has only a termination condition to evaluate. The difference is that it is evaluated at the end of each iteration, rather than at the beginning:

```
do
{

} while(termination condition)
```

The two `while` loop forms also have a scope difference. Variables declared in the termination condition of a `while` loop are visible within the scope of the loop. But in a do loop, there are actually two scopes: the do scope (in the curly braces) and the `while` scope.

The result is that any variables declared in the while portion—the termination condition—of a do loop are not visible to the scope in the curly braces and vice versa.

The following example demonstrates both while loop forms.

```
int i = 0;
while(i < 100)
{
    ++i;
}

int j = 0;
do
{
    ++j;
} while(j < 100);
```

In practice, the standard while loop is used much more frequently than the do loop form. Which you choose to use depends on your circumstances. For example, a do loop should never be used if there is a chance that the termination condition could evaluate to true before the first iteration. Doing so could open the door for some bad bugs. On the other hand, anywhere you can use a do loop, you can use a while loop. In practice though, the do loop is generally used when you know for sure that at least one iteration will run. It's more a way of expressing the intent of the code than of any technical necessity of choosing do over while.

## foreach Loops

The foreach loop is another extremely popular D feature. Not every language has adopted the foreach loop, but it is popping up in more and more modern languages.

A foreach loop is essentially a more efficient for, specialized for the case when you want to visit each element in an array or other container. The idea is that the loop automatically visits every element in a container without you needing to give it any expressions to evaluate, other than a place to store the current element and a container to iterate. A *container* can be a static, dynamic, or associative array. In other words, D works with all three types right out of the box, allowing you to automatically iterate over any type of array and visit each element it contains. You can add this functionality to your own data types as well with a special operator overload, as you'll see in Chapter 3.

A foreach declaration looks like this:

```
foreach([index], value; container) { }
```

where value is a variable that will hold the current element, and container is the array being iterated. index is an optional value that will be assigned the array index, or sequence position, of the current element.

The loop operates in order, from front to back, and executes one iteration for each element in the container. After all of the elements have been iterated, the loop exits.

One of the great things about the foreach loop is that the type of value can be inferred automatically from the type of container, so you don't need to specify the type in the declaration of value.

Here are a few examples of using the foreach loop:

```
int[] x = [0, 1, 2, 3, 4, 5];

// This version specifies the type.
foreach(int y; x)
{
    // Do something with y.
}

// This version uses automatic type inference.
foreach(y; x)
{
    // Do something with y.
}

// This version uses the optional index, and automatic type inference for both
// the index and the value.
foreach(i, y; x)
{
    // Do something with y and x.
}
```

In addition to the standard foreach, D supports foreach_reverse, which does the same thing, except it iterates the container in reverse, from back to front. This is quite handy for implementing custom containers, for iterating the most recent items added to a queue, as an alternative to the reverse property of arrays, and for handling other special cases where you might need to start an iteration from the rear of a container.

# The goto Statement

Those of you familiar with programming language debates are well aware of the goto statement's controversial history. The father of D, Walter Bright, happens to fall into the camp that finds goto useful and, as such, it has found a place in the language.

goto jumps from one point in the program to another point that is marked by a *label*. Older programming languages literally allowed you to jump to any labeled location in the program, which undoubtedly is the major source of early criticism. Modern languages are more restrictive, however, and allow you to jump only to a label in the current scope.

A *label* is an identifier that is followed by a colon. When you jump to a label with goto, execution of the program halts at the point where the goto is encountered and picks up again at the instruction immediately following the label.

The following demonstrates the use of goto.

```
void main()
{
    int x = 1;
repeat:     // This is a label.
    x += 1;
    if(x < 3) goto repeat;     // Repeat x+=1 until x is no longer less than 3.
}
```

---

Note ➡ Admittedly, the example here is a horrible application of goto. However, it does demonstrate the use of goto and labels using constructs you have already seen.

---

These days, the goto statement is most commonly used in C to jump to the end of a function in order to clean up multiple resources in case of an error. But even that is not needed in D, as there are other alternatives, which you'll see in the "Error Handling" section later in this chapter. In D, goto should primarily be considered as a backward-compatibility tool for porting C source directly to D. You should probably avoid it in new code.

# Functions

Now that you've seen the basic data types and flow-control constructs, it's time to look at D's function syntax. Functions in D work much as they do in other C-family languages, although they have a few differences that are uniquely D.

There's nothing revolutionary or unusual about declaring functions in D. The syntax is as follows:

```
ReturnType Identifier(ParameterList) { }
```

where:

- `ReturnType` is the type returned by the function, which will be `void` if there is no return value.

- `Identifier` is the name of the function, which follows the identifier guidelines discussed earlier in the chapter, in the "Declarations" section.

- `ParameterList` is a comma-separated list of zero or more variables as type/identifier pairs.

The following shows the anatomy of a function.

```
int myFunction(int a)    // The declaration
{      // The beginning of the function body and a new scope

    return a+1;      // Immediately exits the function, the result of a + 1
                     // being passed to the caller

}      // The end of the function body and scope
```

In this example, `myFunction` is declared to return type `int`. It accepts one parameter of type `int`. And, finally, the implementation returns the value of the expression `a + 1`.

To call a function, use this syntax:

```
functionName(parameters);
```

So to call the sample `myFunction` function and pass it an integer value of 1, you would do this:

```
myFunction(1);
```

Function parameters can have three different modifiers, or storage classes, that affect their behavior:

in: By default, all function parameters are in parameters if no storage class is specified. An in parameter is passed into a function from the call site with whatever value it has been assigned. If you attempt to modify the *value* of an in parameter, the modification is seen locally only and does not affect the variable at the call site. Effectively, an in parameter is a new variable that is a copy of the value of the original.

out: In contrast to in parameters, out parameters are reset to the default initializer of their type, and modifying them does change the value at the call site.

ref: These parameters are a bit of a combination of the other two. They are passed into a function with whatever value has been assigned to them, and any modifications are reflected at the call site. So you can say that ref parameters are another view of the variable at the call site.

---

Caution ➡ In the case of arrays, the *value* of the array is the object that contains the length and the pointer. Changing this in a function will have no effect at the call site. However, if the *contents* of an array parameter are modified inside a function, the changes *will* be seen at the call site, even if the parameter is declared as in.

---

The following is a complete program that shows how all this works.

```
import tango.io.Stdout;

void main()
{
    int x = 1;
    int y = 2;
    int z = 3;

    Stdout.formatln("In main, x: {} y: {} z: {}", x, y, z);

    // Call some function.
    someFunction(x, y, z);

    Stdout.formatln("In main again, x: {} y: {} z: {}", x, y, z);
}

void someFunction(int x, out int y, ref int z)
{
    Stdout.formatln("In someFunction, x: {} y: {} z: {}", x, y, z);
```

```
    x = 10;
    y = 20;
    z = 30;

    Stdout.formatln("In someFunction again, x: {} y: {} z: {}", x, y, z);
}
```

If you compile and execute this program, you should see the following:

```
In main, x: 1 y: 2 z: 3
In someFunction, x: 1 y: 0 z: 3
In someFunction again, x: 10 y: 20 z: 30
In main again, x: 1 y: 20 z: 30
```

You can see quite clearly that y is set to reset 0, the value of int.init, when it is passed to someFunc, since it is declared in the parameter list as out. You can also see that the assignment made to x in someFunc has no effect on the original value of x in the main function, since the parameter x has the default in storage. Finally, the assignment to both y and z affects the original values back in main, because the parameters were declared as out and ref, respectively.

# Error Handling

In C, errors are typically handled by checking for specific error codes after a function call or through the primitive setjmp mechanism. Perhaps the biggest headache with these dated techniques is the freeing of resources—any resources allocated prior to the point of error must be manually deallocated after the error occurs. Modern programming languages provide a more robust means of error handling through a mechanism called *exception handling*, which allows for the guaranteed deallocation of resources. D, too, supports exception handling, but also provides a handy alternative that offers more precise control over when resources are deallocated.

## Throwing Exceptions

Tango provides an Exception class that is used as the base construct for exception handling. You can think of Exception as an object that contains data that describes an error. When an error occurs in a function, a new `Exception` object can be allocated and *thrown* back to the caller. This throwing of an exception bypasses a function's normal return mechanism.

The following example demonstrates how to throw an exception from a function.

```
void trouble()
{
    // Do something here, but throw an exception on error.
    if(someErrorOccurs)
        throw new Exception("We're in trouble!");

    // Any code here will not be executed if the exception is thrown.
}
```

Here, if the `if` condition evaluates to true, the `throw` statement is executed and causes the function to immediately exit, skipping the execution of any code following the `throw`. The exception will be pushed back to the caller. If the caller ignores the exception, it will be pushed up the call stack until it is handled. By default, all D programs include a top-level exception handler, which *catches* any unhandled exceptions that make it all the way back to the `main` method. This causes any string message associated with the exception to be printed to the console and the program to exit. In the next section, you'll see how to handle, or catch, an exception.

## Catching Exceptions

When you call a function that you know can potentially throw an exception, it's generally a good idea to try to handle that exception at the call site. This will allow you to determine how the program should respond. In some cases, you might want to abort execution immediately; in other situations, you might want to try an alternative operation or ignore the exception altogether. Exceptions are handled via constructs called try/catch/finally blocks.

The first step in handling an exception is to enclose the function call in a try block. try blocks do not work alone, however, and must be followed by a `catch` block, a `finally` block, or both. In the declaration of a `catch` block, you must specify the type of exception you are interested in catching. For our purposes, we'll use the `Exception` object that is available in the default namespace, so you don't need to import any special modules to use it. Inside the `catch` block, you can implement the code you need to respond to the exception. The following example demonstrates this.

```
try
{
    trouble();
```

```
}
catch(Exception e)
{
    // Here you can access e like any other variable, but it is invisible outside
    // the scope of the catch block. If you want, you can 'rethrow' the
    // exception using the throw statement, or return from the function. We'll
    // return for simplicity's sake.
    return;
}
```

One problem with catch blocks is what to do about the code that follows them. If the proper response to the exception is to abort the current function, either via a return statement or by rethrowing the exception, then the code that follows the catch block will not be executed. Sometimes, this is unacceptable, particularly if you need to deallocate any resources that were allocated prior to entering the try/catch blocks. You would need to duplicate the deallocation inside the catch block and after it. That's where finally blocks come in handy.

A finally block must follow either a try or a catch. Any code inside a finally block is guaranteed to execute, whether or not an exception is thrown, and whether or not a thrown exception is caught, as the following example shows.

```
try
{
    trouble();
}
catch(Exception e)
{
    return;
}
finally
{
    // Even if an exception is caught above and the return statement executed,
    // any code in this finally block will still execute before the current
    // function returns.
}
```

---

Caution ➡ try, catch, and finally blocks create a new scope. Any variable declarations inside of one will be invisible to the outside.

---

## Using a scope Statement

finally blocks are great for cleaning up resources, but using them isn't always feasible. When you cannot ensure that the finally block is the last piece of code in a function, you still may need to duplicate code. D's solution to this problem is the scope statement.

You've seen the word *scope* used throughout this chapter in reference to the grouping and visibility of variables and functions. A scope statement is a built-in language feature that you can use to guarantee the execution of a block of code when the current scope exits. A scope can exit either because the end of the scope has been reached through normal execution or because an exception has been thrown. By using a scope statement, you can tell the compiler that a block of code should be executed only when the current scope exists normally, only when an exception is thrown, or when either condition occurs.

The following example demonstrates all three uses of the scope statement.

```
void main()
{
    scope(success) doSomethingOnSuccess();
    scope(failure) doSomethingOnFailure();
    scope(exit)
    {
        doSomethingAlways();
        doSomethingElse();
    }
    // Put your code here.
}
```

Here, the first scope statement will execute only if the current scope—in this case, the main function—exits normally. The second statement will execute only if the current scope exits due to an exception being thrown. The last statement will execute when the current scope exits, regardless of the reason. As you can see, scope statements are a powerful mechanism that can be used to make your code more robust and secure.

This completes our tour of D fundamentals. We've covered a wide range of topics, from basic declarations to error handling. You've learned enough to get your own D programs up and running, but you would be restricted to a subset of D's capabilities. The next chapter opens up more options related to the objected-oriented features of D.

Bell, et al.

# CHAPTER 3

# D's Object-Oriented Features

All the programming languages in the C family provide a way to encapsulate data and operations through the simple struct or the more complex class. D includes support for both classes and structs, but the rules that govern their usage may not be what you are used to from other C languages. For example, D structs are similar to those found in C++ in that they may have methods, but unlike C++ structs, they may not be extended through inheritance. Classes in D are similar to those found in Java in that only single inheritance is supported. Also as in Java, a D class may implement multiple interfaces.

While structs and classes are the main means to encapsulate in D, the language provides a default encapsulation through modules: one per source file. You can often put this fact to good use in cases where structs or classes may not entirely fit the bill. In addition, how you place your other entities in modules (and organize your modules in packages) can affect, or be affected by, protection attributes.

This chapter starts with a discussion of the module. Putting data declarations and functions in multiple source files is enough for basic grouping, and enables the implementation of access protection and namespace encapsulation. Next up, you will read about the struct, which lets you group data, easily access and pass data to C libraries, map data to hardware, and if strictly necessary, emulate some aspects of object-oriented programming.

Following this, you'll be introduced to the struct's big brother, the class. The class is the main mechanism in D to let you employ an object-oriented programming style. By using inheritance, you can build complex type hierarchies, extend the functionality of the superclasses, and have the correct methods in your selected subclass executed.

The next subject of this chapter is the interface. By letting your classes implement defined D interfaces, you can fully separate your application's interfaces from the implementation, making the creation of pluggable third-party implementations a trivial task. It's also commonly considered good practice to separate design from implementation.

Finally, we'll discuss operator overloading. You'll learn how you can overload a variety of D's operators so they can be used with both structs and classes in a manner that you define.

# Modules

You learned some of the basics of D modules in Chapter 1. Here, we are going to expand on that introduction. To recap, each D source file is also called a *module* and is an entity that can be addressed through the language. For most purposes, a module can be seen as a simple, static class.

When you want to access symbols in one module from another module, you can import the other module in its entirety or import only the symbols in which you are interested.

---

Note ➡ A *symbol* is any part of the code that may need to be referenced elsewhere in the generated executable. Typical examples are variables, function names, and the names of user-defined types.

---

Modules can be initialized, used to control access to code, and grouped in packages for further access options. The initialization of modules is usually part of the program startup and is covered in Chapter 4. A *package* is the set of modules contained in any given directory. The name of the package corresponds to the name of this directory.

## Naming Modules

In Chapter 1, you learned that a module name can be declared in code. The module declaration must be the first thing to appear in the source file (with the exception of comments), as in this example:

```
module Time;
```

If a module declaration is not present, the compiler will automatically use the name of the source file as the module name. For example, if the source file is `Time.d`, the module will be named `Time`. In theory, this default behavior is fine for simple applications that do not have a complex module hierarchy. In practice, you should always explicitly name your modules, particularly in large projects and in libraries that you intend other programmers to use.

When you group modules into packages, you must take the package hierarchy into account in the module declaration. Just as the module itself has a one-to-one correlation with the source file, a D package correlates with the directory structure. If your top-level source directory is named `src`, all modules in that directory should contain module declarations such as in the preceding Time example. Modules in any subdirectories must contain the name of the subdirectory in the module declaration, using dot (.) notation to separate the names. For example, the module declaration in the file src/tango/time/Time.d will look like this:

```
module tango.time.Time;
```

Here, the Time module is part of the tango.time package.

## Importing Other Modules

When you start using functions, classes, and other elements in multiple modules, you will need to import the relevant symbols into the module where they are used. An import statement is needed by the compiler so that it knows where to find the symbols you want to use.

D provides a fairly extensive set of import options, including basic, renamed, static, and selective imports. Some of these options can be combined.

### Basic Imports

A basic import is the most common type. The following snippet imports all the symbols in the file tango/time/Time.d:

```
import tango.time.Time;
```

Basic imports have private visibility by default. You learned about private and public imports in Chapter 1. For a public import, prefix the import statement with the public keyword:

```
public import tango.time.Time;
```

The imported symbols will now be propagated into modules importing this module. A public import is most commonly used for setting up systemwide symbols.

---

Note ➡ A private import will still pull in symbols from public imports in the imported module.

---

You can import multiple modules in one import statement by separating each module name with a comma, as in the following example:

```
import tango.io.FilePath,
       tango.io.FileConduit;
```

## Renamed Imports

By renaming an import, you effectively create a namespace through which to access the imported symbols. For instance, the following line will make the symbols in Integer accessible only through the name Int:

```
import Int = tango.text.convert.Integer;
```

If Integer has a function called format, you must use the following syntax to call it:

```
Int.format();
```

You should use renamed imports in two particular cases:

- When the API of the module consists of free functions that have short names that may not be self-documenting out of context. By renaming the import, you will always use the functions through a namespace you've specified.

- When the symbols imported from one module conflict with symbols imported from another. By renaming the import, you will also rename the imported symbols so that they no longer conflict.

In practice, it may make sense to use renamed imports as often as possible in order to future-proof your code.

## Selective Imports

If you use only a small number of symbols from an imported module, you can import only those symbols using a selective import:

```
import tango.text.Util : strip, trim;
```

This line implies that the module Util has at least the symbols strip and trim, and these will be made directly available in the importing module. Any other symbols in the imported module will not be visible.

You can combine selective imports with renamed imports in two ways: you can create a new namespace for the module from which you are selectively importing, and you can rename the selected symbols. The following line shows an example of both techniques:

```
import TextUtils = tango.text.Util : clean = strip;
```

This creates a new `TextUtils` namespace and renames the symbol `strip` to `clean`. Assuming `strip` is a function, you would now call it like so:

```
TextUtils.clean;
```

### Static Imports

Another technique for avoiding name collisions when importing modules is to use the `static` keyword. This ensures that you always need to use the fully qualified name of any symbol you access from that module. Here is an example:

```
static import tango.text.Util;
// Using the function strip
tango.text.Util.strip();
```

## Accessing Variables in Module Scope

A module is both a code container by itself and a container for other code containers like structs and classes. You may encounter situations where you have variables in your module scope that you want to access in your class. This is generally not a problem. However, if you also have local variables in your class or struct with the same names as the variables in module scope that you want to use, you need to distinguish those variables. You do this by prefixing the variable name with the global scope operator . (a dot).

In the following example, `outerState` returns the value of the variable `state` found in the module scope, not the one in the class scope:

```
module Parser;

int state;

class Parser {
    int state;
    int outerState() { return .state; }
}
```

## Creating Unit Tests

D goes a step beyond most mainstream languages when it comes to making it easy for you to create tests and contracts directly in your code. Support for unit tests (both for test-driven development processes and regression testing) is built into the D programming language.

The following example shows a simple unit test asserting the return value of the function `square`:

```
unittest {
    assert (square(4) == 16);
}
```

A `unittest` block can have as many asserts as necessary, and there is no limit to how many unit tests a source file can have.

To run your unit tests, compile your program with the -unittest (DMD) switch. They will be run in order of appearance before `main` is executed. If any assertion is false, the unit test run will abort.

If you need to modify or control how unit tests are run, you can set a unit test handler for your program via `moduleUnitTester` in `tango.core.Runtime`.

---

Caution ➡ You cannot import other modules inside your unit tests. If your tests require different modules than the production code of your module, you should import these in a versioned block. The Tango style guide recommends wrapping these imports and the unit test itself in a debug(UnitTest) block, which also avoids contaminating your application with Tango's unit tests.

---

# Structs and Unions

If you have programmed in C or C++, you are familiar with the *struct* and its close cousin, the *union*. The struct is a simple value type. It lets you group data and functions so that fields that are likely to be used in conjunction with each other are kept close in memory, and functions operating on the data are available through the same declared name.

---

Caution ➡ D's structs are not equal to those of C and C++. Unlike in C, D structs may contain member functions. Unlike C++, D does not support polymorphism within structs.

---

Structs can be well suited for object-oriented programming, when using composition instead of inheritance for building your types. However, you cannot derive subclasses from structs or use interfaces with them. Otherwise, structs are excellent to use for plain-old data objects. The fact that they are allocated on the stack instead of the heap is often considered a major boon. In Tango, Time is implemented as a struct instead of a class for this exact reason.

In D, you would use structs in the following cases:

- When you are interfacing with C libraries and operating systems that have a C interface whose functions take structs as input arguments or return structs.

- If you are programming directly against hardware where the contents of a struct can be mapped directly over a memory range, input or output.

- When you are encapsulating data in your everyday D programming, and the overhead of classes is unacceptable. This is not a choice you should base on performance reasons alone, as certain benefits pertaining to classes and interfaces will be lost.

In essence, a struct is a bag of bits with optional functions that operate on them. The bit layout is guaranteed, meaning that you can create exact bit copies of your structs.

## Defining Structs

When you define a struct, it's usually a matter of naming it, and then specifying its data fields and operations. However, you can further customize it by specifying the byte boundary it is to be aligned on, how it is to be allocated, and any invariants or unit tests you may need. An *invariant* is a built-in test that guarantees that an object maintains a consistent state between operations, as discussed in the "Invariants" section later in this chapter. Structs can also have static data that can be initialized and cleaned up with static constructors and destructors.

Here is an example of defining a simple struct:

```
struct Time {
    uint hour;
    int timeZone;
    bool usingAM;

    int time() {
        if (usingAM && hour > 12) return hour - 12;
        else return hour;
```

```
    }
}
```

Usually, you don't need to align the struct contents when coding in D, but you may in some special circumstances, such as when the struct is defined for use with a particular C library. Alignment places the struct members on a given byte boundary.

You can prefix `struct` members with the `align` attribute to make sure the alignment you need is the alignment you get. Using `align` by itself indicates that the default alignment should be used. Using `align` with a number, as in the following example, will deviate the alignment from the default.

```
struct S {
    align(4) int a;
    align(4) int b;
}
```

The exact meaning of the integer (4 in the example) depends on the compiler. With DMD, it is simply ignored.

The next example does not actually align members, but instead packs the struct for binary compatibility across platforms.

```
align(1) struct S { . . . }
```

## Defining Unions

Unions are useful in those cases where you need to keep track of a value that can be represented as different data types during the lifetime of the program. Unions are most often found in low-level code, where they are mainly used to save memory.

---

Caution ➡ Unions let you subvert the type system in the language, and are thus inherently unsafe to use. Make sure you really need unions before using them.

---

For example, in error reporting, an error can initially be represented as a number, but later, after a lookup in an error message table, can become accessible as a descriptive text. It achieves this by making its members mutually exclusive, but otherwise appears to operate in the same way as a struct. Here is an example of a union that represents an error:

```
union Error {
```

```
    int errorCode;
    char[] errorMessage;
}
```

In the example, the union `Error` can be initialized to have a value only for either `errorCode` or `errorMessage`, not both. If the members are of different sizes, the union will always be initialized to the size of the biggest member. Unused space will be padded with zeros.

If you assign a value of type `char[]` to a variable of type `Error`, `errorMessage` will be set to that value and `errorCode` zeroed. It is your responsibility to keep track of which member currently holds a value.

# Initializing Structs

Structs are inherently value types—just collections of data fields—so it makes sense to make it syntactically easy for you to initialize them. You can initialize a struct either statically or dynamically.

## Static Initialization

You can statically initialize a struct in two ways in D, one of which also applies to unions.

One initialization method involves naming the members that you want to give initial values followed by the values they should have, as in the following example:

```
static Time t = { hour:7, timeZone:-2 };
```

This will declare a static variable `t` of type `Time`, where `t.hour` and `t.timeZone` are initialized to 7 and –2, respectively. If the definition of the struct contains more fields than those handled in the initialization, the unhandled fields will be initialized to either the type's default initializer or the initializer set in the definition of the struct. This technique can also be used with unions, in which case you initialize only one field.

You can also initialize all members of a struct by giving each a value in order of declaration:

```
static Time t = { 7, -2 };
```

This will initialize the first two fields of the struct to 7 and –2, respectively, whereas any following fields will be initialized to either the type's default initializer or the initializer set for a given field in the definition of the struct. This technique cannot be used with unions.

## Dynamic Initialization

As of D 1.0, structs don't have constructors. However, you can still dynamically initialize them.

One method for dynamic initialization involves using an existing value of the same type, such as in the following example:

```
// Given a defined struct Time
Time t;
t.hour = 3;
Time at = t;
```

Here, at is initialized with the data in t. In other words, the values of the fields in t will be copied into the fields of at, such that at.hour will be initialized to 3.

One way you can simulate a constructor is by adding a static opCall method to the struct definition. This method accepts your initialization parameters and returns an instance of the struct. Here is an example:

```
static Time opCall(int time) {
    Time t;
    t.hour = time;
    return t;
}
```

Now this opCall will function as a constructor. Here's how it looks when used:

```
Time t = Time(3);
```

## Struct Literals

You can create a struct value and pass it directly to a function taking that type, or use it to initialize a variable, by using struct literals. This approach is syntactically the same as a call to opCall, in that it will work only as long as you haven't overridden opCall in your struct. Here is an example:

```
void setTime(Time t);
setTime( Time(1, 2) );
```

The arguments in the struct literal will initialize the first fields in the struct in that order. If your struct has more fields than covered by the arguments, they will be initialized to their default values.

### Struct Allocation

Unless you say differently, a struct is treated by the compiler as any basic type and will be allocated on the stack. If you need to retain structs—keep them around and pass them to other functions not living in the scope where they were created—you need to allocate them on the heap. The following statement will allocate the struct on the heap (or invoke a customized allocator), giving you a pointer to the data:

```
Time * dt = new Time;
```

When allocating a struct on the heap, accessing the members of dt is syntactically no different from when you have allocated the struct on the stack.

## Using Struct Properties

As with other types, structs have some properties built in for your use, as listed in Table 3-1.

*Table 3-1. Struct Properties*

| Property | Description |
| --- | --- |
| sizeof | Returns the struct's size in bytes |
| alignof | Returns the size boundary on which the struct needs to be aligned |
| tupleof | Returns a tuple of the struct's fields |

In addition, you can use the offsetof property on each of the fields to find the offset from the beginning of the struct. The first field has offset 0.

# Classes

Object-oriented programming is mainly supported in D through its classes and interfaces. Classes go much further than the composition-only capabilities of the struct. Their features include inheritance, polymorphism, virtual functions, and an identity. Classes in D are reference types, as they are in Java and unlike in C++, where they are value types. If you are familiar with the object-oriented programming features available in Java or C++, you will find that D's corresponding features are similar.

## Class Definition and Instantiation

A simple class definition can be syntactically identical to a struct definition except for the keyword itself. Indeed, in D 1.0, only constructors, destructors, and inheritance-related features are available exclusively to classes and not to structs. For example, you could transform the earlier Time struct into a class as follows:

```
class Time {
    uint h;
    int tz;

    uint hour() { return h; }

    this(uint hour, int timeZone) {
```

```
        this.h = hour;
        this.tz = timeZone;
    }
}
```

This example shows the class `Time` with the (public, by default) fields h and tz, and the method hour (which returns the value of h for the instance on which the method is called). this is a special method and is the class's constructor. Here, the constructor sets the instance's fields to the values passed through its arguments. Within a class, the keyword this can be used to discern symbols in the class scope from the parameter names and represents the this pointer, the instance itself.

After you have defined your class, you'll want to create instances of it in your code. This is done with the new expression, as in this example:

```
File f = new File("tango/io/File.d");
```

The example creates an instance f of type File by calling File's constructor—in this case, a constructor that takes a string with the path to the file to open. In addition to executing the constructor, memory is allocated for the class, and a reference to the instance is returned (and, in this case, assigned to f).

By default, all class instances are allocated on the heap. Sometimes, it may be convenient to allocate a class instance on the stack instead. You can do this by using the scope attribute in your variable declaration, as follows:

```
scope f = new File("tango/io/File.d");
```

Here, because the scope attribute is a storage class, the type of the variable can be omitted for automatic type inference. The important point is that, in addition to being allocated on the stack, the destructor of the instance f will also be called automatically when the current visibility scope in which it resides (a function body or while loop, for example) exits. When you use object instances that are short-lived, this is a handy technique to ensure that any resources they use are automatically cleaned up via their destructors.

# Invariants

Classes are generally used to encapsulate data and operations that belong together, just like structs. Classes and structs are often a good match to model abstract or more physical objects in the real world. Typically, these objects have valid ranges for their internal state, and the rules that specify these valid states are called *invariants*. As long as the tests for these rules pass, you can say that the object is in a valid state.

In D, invariants are part of the language's *design by contract* features, letting you create runtime tests for the state of your struct, union, or class. The invariants are checked before and after every method call when the program is compiled in nonrelease mode. If the assertion is false, an AssertException will be thrown.

This following shows how to give the Time class an invariant for the value of the month property.

```
class Time {
    private uint month; // 0 is January, 11 December
    invariant() {
        assert ( month < 12 );
    }
}
```

The invariant in this example checks whether the month property is within legal bounds. It cannot have a value that does not represent one of the 12 months of the year.

Use invariants to help verify that your data is in a valid state. You can explicitly call the invariant for your objects as follows:

```
assert (o);
```

In this line, o is an object reference. The compiler transforms this into code for running the invariant of that class.

Encapsulated entities such as classes, structs, and unions, can have only one invariant.


# Inheritance

When creating new types in D via the class system, inheritance is the most powerful mechanism. *Inheritance* means that you create types that inherit state and operations from existing classes, and then customize the functionality. You are most likely to use inheritance to take advantage of polymorphism, which is detailed in the next section.

Whenever you define a class, it is already implicitly a *subclass* of Object, but you can generally ignore that fact. It will be considered a *superclass* if it is inherited by some other class, and a *base class* if it doesn't explicitly inherit any class. Multiple inheritance is not supported in D; a class can have only one direct superclass. However, a class can implement several interfaces, and an interface can have several superinterfaces. The interface construct is discussed in its own section later in this chapter.

Defining a new class by inheriting a superclass results in all public and protected members (whether data fields or methods) in the superclass becoming visible in the subclass. In addition, the subclass can have its own fields and methods that will be invisible to the superclass.

The following example is an abbreviated version of the FileConduit class in Tango, which inherits DeviceConduit:

```
class FileConduit : DeviceConduit {
    private PathView path_;
    PathView path() { return path_; }
}
```

This example adds the path method, which returns the value of the private field path_. The private field name ends with an underscore so that it will not conflict with the public method.

When creating a subclass, you may need to explicitly use a member in the superclass (this is especially common when overriding, as discussed in the "Overriding Methods" section later in this chapter). A reference to a class's superclass is available by using the super keyword.

To further complement the behavior reached through inheritance, you can use various attributes and techniques to change or augment the behavior of the methods in the superclass when subclassing, as discussed in the "Polymorphism" section later in this chapter.

You can protect your class from being further subclassed by declaring it to be final, as follows:

```
final class FilePath { . . . }
```

In class inheritance, abstract classes (which are not meant to be instantiated) play a special role. They can be normal classes declared abstract to avoid instantiation, a partial implementation, or a viable alternative to the use of a single interface. Abstract classes are covered in more detail in the discussion of interfaces later in this chapter.

# Polymorphism

When using a particular class instance in your program, you know that it exposes certain methods and properties. If the creator of the class has done his job, each exposed method and property is documented so that any return values and side effects are understood. When you call a class method, you usually have a reasonable idea what effect it will have on your program. Consider the InputStream instance used in the produce method in the following example:

```
class MyProducer {
    void[] buffer;
    void produce(InputStream data) {
        data.read(buffer);
        data.clear.close;
    }
}
```

Here, instances of MyProducer will call the read, clear, and close methods of an InputStream instance. The call to each method is based on the knowledge of which parameters, if any, the methods accept and the types they return. For example, the clear method returns the InputStream instance it was called on, enabling the chained call to close. The caller also knows what each method is supposed to accomplish. However, the caller does not know how each method of InputStream is implemented.

The instance of InputStream that is passed to the produce method could be one of a number of implementations, and MyProducer would never know the difference. In object-oriented terms, this is called *polymorphism*.

With polymorphism, a common interface (here, meaning the set of methods exposed by a class or interface type) can be implemented by multiple classes, each overriding or overloading methods to provide customized behavior. Overriding and overloading, as well as the other features of D that facilitate the use of polymorphism, are discussed in the following sections.

## Protection Attributes

Protection, or visibility, attributes were introduced in Chapter 1 in the context of modules. The basic meaning is the same when you use them in classes: they control access to the class. As mentioned earlier, all fields and methods are public by default unless another protection attribute is explicitly specified. The following attributes are available:

- public: This is the default protection and means that anyone can access the member through an import.

- private: If you declare a field or method to be private, it will be visible only in the enclosing class; neither users of the class nor subclasses will have access to it.

---

Note ➡ You can access any field or method from an entity within the same module (for instance if you create a subclass in the same module), even if it is declared as private. This can be seen as an implicit implementation of the friend feature found in C++.

---

- protected: If you want a class to have methods that could or should be called only by its subclasses, use the protected attribute. Apart from being visible to subclasses, protected members are the same as private ones.

- package: This attribute extends protected visibility so that the members are visible only in all modules that are in the same package.

- export: The storage class export is an extension to public protection. It means that the symbol also can be accessed from outside the program executable.

The package and export attributes are not commonly used. The export option would apply only to dynamic libraries and their exported symbols, and on non-Windows platforms, this is usually the default behavior.

## Overloading Methods

Overloading a method in a class is generally governed by the same rules as for functions in the module scope or in a struct. As public and protected methods are visible in subclasses, however, you may find that you need to overload one of those methods in the subclass. This turns into a special case for the compiler's name lookup mechanism.

You may think that the methods with the same name from the superclass are still visible in the subclass, but they are not. Otherwise, you might rely on a method in a subclass, only to get inexplicable errors when a method with the same name is added to the superclass (and preferred by the compiler due to an implicit conversion).

If you are sure that you want to make the methods in the superclass visible to the subclass along with its overloads, you must specify this explicitly. Here is an example of overloading taken from tango.sys.Pipe, where various methods of DeviceConduit are brought into Pipe's namespace:

```
class Pipe : DeviceConduit {
        alias DeviceConduit.copy        copy;
        alias DeviceConduit.read        read;
}
```

## Overriding Methods

Overriding is often confused with overloading, but instead of adding methods with a common name taking other input parameters, *overriding* means to reimplement a method in a subclass. Overriding a method can totally disable the functionality in the superclass, or it can extend it by calling it via the super reference. Here is an example:

```
class FileConduit : DeviceConduit {
    private void closeFile() { . . . }

    override void close() {
        super.close();
        closeFile();
    }
}
```

This example calls `close` in the superclass before adding to that functionality by calling the subclass's private method `closeFile`.

Using the `override` attribute is not mandatory when overriding in D 1.0, but is highly recommended for self-documentation purposes and protection from the case where a subclass may inadvertently override a method in the superclass. The effect of the attribute is that the compiler will complain (when warnings are turned on) if there is no method to override.

You can also give overridden fields and methods in your classes protection attributes that differ from those in the superclass as a means to refine the inheritance. Thus, you can protect what is public in the superclass or expose what is protected. However, doing this is considered very bad practice, and should be used only as a last resort to fix a broken design.

## Covariant Return Types

In a class hierarchy, you may find the need for overridden methods that return types tied to the current level in the hierarchy. For example, consider a class `DataInput` that is a subclass of `InputStream`. The `InputStream.clear` method is defined to return an instance of `InputStream`. However, in the `DataInput` class, it is possible to declare an overridden version of the method that explicitly returns an instance of `DataInput`:

```
class DataInput : InputStream
{
    public DataInput clear()
    {
        super.clear;
    }
}
```

This is a feature called *covariant return types*.

D doesn't discern overloads by return type, thus your overrides in the subclass will also be used when you change the return types to fit the new class. By doing this, you will more easily avoid situations where your received reference needs to be cast to the type of the subclass. This is not a problem in the opposite direction, since a subclass can always be implicitly converted to its superclass.

## Final Methods

In the cases where you need to protect the methods in your class from being overridden in subclasses, declare them as final. The compiler will then generate an error whenever an attempt is made to override those methods. An added benefit of making a method final is that the compiler can mark it as nonvirtual if the method itself does not override a method in a superclass. This makes all calls to it direct instead of via the virtual table.

## Static Members

In object-oriented programming, you usually use instances of your defined classes. However, you still may want a class to contain data or operations that do not depend on an instance. In the following example from Tango, SocketConduit keeps a list of previously allocated conduits so that one of them can be reused later. freelist is a static field in the class, whereas the allocate method is a static method.

```
class SocketConduit : Conduit {
        private static SocketConduit freelist;
        private SocketConduit            next;

        package static synchronized SocketConduit allocate ()
        {
                SocketConduit s;

                if (freelist)
                   {
                   s = freelist;
                   freelist = s.next;
                   }
                else
                   . . .
                return s;
        }
}
```

Accessing the static freelist variable is not possible from outside the module, as it is private. Non-private fields can be accessed through the class name. In the example, SocketConduit static methods, like allocate, cannot reference non-static members of the class. Instead, they are mainly used for operations that are related to the class, and therefore grouped under its name. Analogous to non-private fields, static methods are called through the class name, as in this example:

```
SocketConduit sc = SocketConduit.allocate();
```

This example gets a `SocketConduit` instance from `allocate`. `allocate` has package visibility, and so cannot be used outside `tango.net`.

## Constructors and Destructors

As mentioned earlier, the class's constructor is a special method named `this`. A return type is not specified (it is always a reference to the constructed object). A class constructor can be overloaded like any other method or function, and can call overloaded constructors or those in a superclass. Here is an example:

```
class SC : C {
    private int i;
    this (int i) { this(i, true); }
    this (int i, bool b) { super (i, b); . . . }
}
```

In this example, a default value is passed on for the `bool` parameter to the main constructor, if the simpler overload is used. This particular class is a subclass, and the constructor makes use of the constructor in the superclass by calling the special method `super`, which is the superclass's constructor.

You will not find the destructor in D very useful compared to the one in C++, given that the garbage collector collects all heap-allocated memory by default. As such, destructors are useful only for cleaning up other types of resources, like file handles, and then only in scoped classes where a deterministic destruction is guaranteed. Object lifetime is discussed in more detail in Chapter 4. A destructor is defined by adding a ~ (tilde) in front of `this`.

## Nested Classes

D allows you to define and use nested classes in both functions and classes. They are inherently tied to their scope, although they can be public and thus visible from outside the nesting class, given certain limitations.

To construct an instance of an inner class from outside the enclosing class, you need to use an instance of the enclosing class and call the constructor of the nested class on that. Here is an example:

```
class Outer {
    class Nested { }
}

Outer o = new Outer;
Outer.Nested nested = o.new Nested;
```

A class nested in a function cannot be constructed from outside that function.

If your nested class needs to access the instance of the enclosing class, you can use the outer property of the this pointer of the nested class. If the class is nested in a function, the outer property will be a pointer to the function's stack frame—the part of memory where information about the called functions are kept.

## Anonymous Classes

Many object-oriented design patterns make use of anonymous classes. In D, these are technically nested classes, as they always are created within a function or method. The most common usage is to make implementations of simple interfaces, such as for handling events from peripherals. The following is an example where you can register EventHandler instances using anonymous classes that implement the EventHandler interface:

```
interface EventHandler { void handle(Event); }
void registerHandler(EventHandler eh) { . . . }

registerHandler(
        new class EventHandler {
            void handle(Event e) { e.printDetails(); }
        }
);
```

EventHandler is a simple interface that has one method: handle. In the call to registerHandler, which takes a parameter of type EventHandler, a new class expression is used to implement the interface. Only new, class, and the body are required. An argument list to new (in case of a custom allocator), an argument list to class (for eventual constructors), a superclass, and any number of interfaces are optional. Interfaces are discussed in more detail shortly.

## Class Properties

Classes have only one built-in property for you to use: `tupleof`, which returns a tuple of the class's fields.

In addition, you can use the property `offsetof` on each of the fields to find the offset from the beginning of the class. The first field has offset 0.

The usual way of exposing properties in a class is by implementing getters and setters for its fields. You can call these using normal assignment syntax, making them behave the same as built-in properties, as follows:

```
class File {
    private PathView path_;
    void path(PathView p) { path_ = p; }
    PathView path() { return path_; }
}
```

This example shows a class with a private field `path_`, which has a setter and a getter, both called path. The following demonstrates how the syntax allows for using `path_` as if it were a public field called path.

```
import tango.io.Stdout;
import tango.io.File,
       tango.io.FilePath;
File f = new File;
f.path = new FilePath("tango/io/FilePath.d");
Stdout (f.path);
```

The syntax for custom properties is particularly useful for prototyping classes by using public fields. You can then create getters and setters if the design is sound, without needing to change the code using it. By omitting either the getter or setter, you will effectively make the field write-only or read-only, respectively.

# Interfaces

An *interface* is a collection of operations and the data, how they are organized or encapsulated, and a functional description of how you can use them. In any full-scale project, you can expect to find both public interfaces and internal interfaces, subsystem interfaces, and intermodule interfaces. However, in the context of object-oriented programming, an `interface` type is a different beast.

In D, an interface is much like a class that is missing an implementation. It is often useful to view the interface as a contract between the API user and the implementing party.

An interface in D is conceptually similar to a class, but the methods cannot be implemented, and no constants may be defined. The interface describes only the methods that the implementing class should have. A class can implement any number of interfaces, representing the various facets of functionality that the class has.

## Interface Definition

Here is an example of defining a simple interface:

```
interface InputStream {
        IConduit conduit ();
        uint read (void[] dst);
        void clear ();
}
```

The defined `interface InputStream` from Tango has only the methods `conduit`, `read`, and `clear`. These classes need to be implemented in any class that declares this interface.

## Class Implementation of Interfaces

Interfaces can be a fully abstract view of available functionality and are especially useful when there can be multiple possible implementations. In Tango, the most notable example is the input/output system, where a few formalized interfaces define how you can interact with various streams of data, whether these come from a socket, a file, or a process pipe.

As mentioned previously, it is possible for a class to implement several interfaces. This makes it possible to divide functionality into several interfaces, which may make sense on its own. In Tango, the various conduits implement both `InputStream` and `OutputStream`, as they are bidirectional. They are, however, useful on their own, as when applying filters like compression to the data streams.

It is not possible to instantiate interfaces, but you can have references to class instances through the type of an interface that the class implements.

Interfaces can also inherit other interfaces. Classes implementing the subinterface will need to implement all methods in both the subinterface and the superinterface. The syntax for a class implementing an interface is the same as for inheritance. Here is an example:

```
class FileConduit : DeviceConduit, DeviceConduit.Seek{ . . . }
```

Bell, et al.

This shows the class `FileConduit` inheriting from `DeviceConduit` in addition to implementing the interface `DeviceConduit.Seek`, meaning that `FileConduit` is made seekable.

## Abstract Classes

An abstract class is, in its simplest form, just a class that has been declared with the abstract keyword. This creates a class that you won't be allowed to instantiate, such as the following:

```
abstract class Conduit { . . . }
```

In Tango, `Conduit` is not explicitly declared abstract, but is implicitly abstract. This happens whenever you create a class that has methods that are not implemented, either by just providing the signature followed by a semicolon or by declaring a class to implement an interface, and not actually implementing the methods declared in it. You can declare a method in a class to be abstract, too, for the sake of documentation, but it is not required for abstract methods.

The next example is an actual abstract method in `Conduit`:

```
abstract uint write (void [] src);
```

You will typically use abstract classes when you have an interface that you want to be implemented, but you want to have default implementations for some or all of the methods.

---

Note ➡ When it comes to inheritance, abstract classes are restricted in the same way as full classes, meaning that your classes can have only one abstract superclass.

---

# Operator Overloading

D has many operators, all with a well-defined behavior for the basic types or in basic situations. When defining either structs or classes, many of the operations described by these operators can be overloaded.

The arithmetic operations are available for mathematical programmers to use on classes like `Matrix` and `Vector`. The other overloadable operators, such as those for comparison, can be more generally applicable. In Tango, you will find, among other operator overloads, the comparison operator implemented for `Text`, and `BitArray`, typically sortable data types. The equality operator is implemented for a wider selection. The special function call operator is also widely used to simplify usage of common operations.

The overloadable operators have a predefined method name attached to them. By implementing one in your new type and using the operator in conjunction with instances of the given type, the operation will be executed as you intended.

The operators that can be overloaded can be categorized as unary, binary, and special operators, as discussed in the following sections.

## Unary Operators

A unary operator does not take any parameters, and the method representing it is called on the instance on which the operator is used. Table 3-2 lists the unary operators available for overloading, where o represents the object instance where the overloaded operator is implemented.

*Table 3-2. Unary Operators Available for Overloading*

| Operator | Method Name | Example |
|---|---|---|
| Neg | opNeg | -o |
| Pos | opPos | +o |
| Complement | opCom | ~o |
| Increment | opPostInc | o++ |
| Decrement | opPostDec | o-- |
| Cast | opCast | cast(C)o |

When any of the operators listed in Table 3-2 are used on an object instance, overloading the special method for the given operator, the expression is rewritten to this:

o.opMethod();

The first five operators listed in Table 3-2 should normally change the state of the instance, and as such, a return value may not always make sense. However, you can implement the operators with a return value, such as to get a numerical value representing the changed state.

The opCast operator needs to have a return type different from the one to the class or type where it is implemented. It is used to cast the instance to some other value. For example, an instance of Integer can be cast to the basic type int. D does not allow overloads on return types, meaning you can implement only one opCast per class (the returned type is the type to which you cast the object).

# Binary Operators

Binary operators are called on one instance, taking some other instance or value as a parameter. Table 3-3 shows binary operators that you can overload in your structs and classes. In the table, o is an instance of the class implementing the operator, and c is a value or instance passed as a parameter.

*Table 3-3. Binary Operators Available for Overloading*

| Operator | Method Name | Example | Right-hand Version |
|---|---|---|---|
| Add | opAdd | o + c | opAdd_r |
| Sub | opSub | o - c | opSub_r |
| Multiply | opMul | o * c | opMul_r |
| Divide | opDiv | o / c | opDiv_r |
| Modulo | opMod | o % c | opMod_r |
| AND | opAnd | o & c | opAnd_r |
| OR | opOr | o & c | opOr_r |
| XOR | opXor | o ^ c | opXor_r |
| Shift left | opShl | o << c | opShl_r |
| Shift right | opShr | o >> c | opShr_r |
| Unsigned shift right | opUShr | o >>> c | opUShr_r |

*(Continued)*

| Operator | Method Name | Example | Right-hand Version |
|---|---|---|---|
| Concatenate | opCat | o ~ c | opCat_r |
| Equals | opEquals | o == c | |
| Unequal | opEquals | o != c | |
| Less than | opCmp | o < c | |
| Less than or equal | opCmp | o <= c | |
| Greater than | opCmp | o > c | |
| Greater than or equal | opCmp | o >= c | |
| Assign | opAssign | o = c | |
| Add and assign | opAddAssign | o += c | |
| Subtract and assign | opSubAssign | o -= c | |
| Multiply and assign | opMulAssign | o *= c | |
| Divide and assign | opDivAssign | o /= c | |
| Modulo and assign | opModAssign | o %= c | |
| AND and assign | opAndAssign | o &= c | |
| OR and assign | opOrAssign | o |= c | |
| XOR and assign | opXorAssign | o ^= c | |
| Shift left and assign | opShlAssign | o <<= c | |
| Shift right and assign | opShrAssign | o >>= c | |
| Unsigned shift right and assign | opUShrAssign | o >>>= c | |
| Concatenate and assign | opCatAssign | o ~= c | |
| In | opIn | c in o | opIn_r |

When any of the binary operators listed in Table 3-3 are used on an object instance, overloading the special method for the given operator, the expression is rewritten to the following:

```
o.opMethod(c);
```

In the case where only the right-hand side version is implemented, the rewrite will be to the following instead:

```
c.opMethod_r(o);
```

If the operator is commutative, the compiler tries to rewrite the other way around.

The binary operators can be overloaded to take different types of parameters (but only one), such that an operator can be used for different types on the right-hand side. Except for the operators opEquals and opCmp, the return value is not required.

---

Note ➡ Both opEquals and opCmp are implemented in Object, thus any implementation you make will be an override. Object's implementation of opCmp creates a runtime error though, so you *must* override it to use it.

---

Both opEquals and opCmp return an int, representing the outcome of the test. In both of these cases, the implementation is used for several operators (see Table 3-3).

opEquals should return either 0 (in case the test for equality is false) or a positive value. The expression is rewritten to the following if you used the != operator:

```
!o.opEquals(c);
```

Similar rules are applied to opCmp, but it should return a positive number if the entity implementing the operator overload has a value greater than the one to which it is compared, negative if it is smaller, and 0 if they are equal. This means the compiler's rewritten expression will produce a result that makes sense to you for the given operator.

opAssign deserves some special mention, as there are some restrictions to the parameter types it can accept. It cannot be implemented such that it can be passed any type that can be implicitly converted to the type of the class implementing the opAssign overload. The reason is that such an overload will conflict with the execution of a normal assignment— that is, a bitwise copy for a struct and assignment of a class reference if the type is a class, such as in this example:

```
O o = new O;
```

# Special Operators

You read about overloading the function call operator, ( ), when we discussed how to initialize structs, earlier in the chapter. Actually, you can overload this operator for both classes and structs, in both static and virtual variations. The special method for it is opCall, although the only difference from other methods is in how it is called. By overloading it, the class name (if static) or instance variable becomes a function name you can use. Tango associates this mechanism with specific library facilities, such as Stdout. The following lines are functionally equivalent:

```
Stdout("Output: ", 2);

Stdout.opCall("Output: ", 2);
```

Stdout is a preinstantiated object of Tango's Print class, where the output stream is the system's standard output channel, and implements the following function:

```
Print print(. . .);
```

This function is then aliased to opCall to make it callable, as shown in the example.

---

Tip ➡ If you have a method that is particularly suitable for opCall (print, for example) you can do alias print opCall; to make that member also callable using an instance of the object directly.

---

The rest of the operators available for overloading are related to operations on arrays, indexing, assigning of elements, and slicing:

- opIndex: This operator can take any number of parameters, where the values passed as arguments are comma-separated values within the square brackets of the indexing operator. opIndex will return a value or reference of the type that the container contains.

- opIndexAssign: This operator is similar to opIndex, with the main difference being that its first parameter is the value being assigned.

- opSlice: The slice operator is the one used in expressions like a[] and a[i..j], and can also be overloaded, both for reading and assignment. opSlice matches the first version if it has no parameters, and the second if it has two parameters matching the types of i and j. You usually want the operator to return an array or similar representing the set of the slice.

- opSliceAssign: This operator takes the assigned value as its first parameter, but is otherwise similar to opSlice.

- opIn: This operator should be implemented to have your type behave as an associative array. It must have the key type as a parameter, and it should return a pointer to an object, or zero if nothing was found.

You would typically implement these operators in your types emulating arrays, such as Vector.

This completes our discussion of D's object-oriented features, from modules to interfaces and overloading and overriding. The next chapter talks about the lifetimes of the D language types.

# CHAPTER 4

# Procedural Lifetime

The D programming language contains value types, pointer types, and reference types. Each type has unique storage attributes and manifests a different functional lifetime. Additionally, type attributes can affect the lifetime of the associated declaration, occasionally in rather unique ways. The aim of this chapter is to explore the lifetime guarantees afforded to each kind of type and to elucidate some of the more specialized language behavior related to the lifetime of reference types.

## D Language Type Classifications

Before diving into the particulars of specific data types, it may be useful to review how types are classified. D language types fall into three main categories:

*Value*: A value type is a type whose data is inextricably linked to the point of declaration. The size needed to store such a type is known at compile time and directly affects the footprint of the function or user-defined type (UDT) in which it is declared. D's basic data types—int, char, float, and so on—are all value types, and each has specific size and storage requirements outlined by the language specification.

*Pointer*: As discussed in Chapter 2, a pointer type is a special kind of value type that represents a memory address. The size needed to store a pointer type is always the size of a memory address on the target system, regardless of the underlying data type to which the pointer refers. Because of this separation between variable and data, the lifetime of a pointer is unrelated to the lifetime of the data to which it refers. Thus, the garbage collection of a pointer variable affects only the address value, and not any underlying data to which the pointer may refer.

*Reference*: A reference type is a special kind of pointer type that does not require the usual machinations to distinguish between operations on the address and operations on the underlying data. Like pointers, however, reference types occupy a small, fixed amount of space at the point of declaration (typically the same amount as a pointer, though this is not required), and the data resides elsewhere. Similarly, when a reference type is garbage-collected, the data or object it references is not, unless the reference type has the `scope` attribute (discussed in Chapter 3).

# Scope and Lifetime

The lifetime of a variable is a function of the scope in which it is declared. If a variable is declared within a function, for example, space will be allocated for that variable when the function is called and will be collected when the function returns. Similarly, variables declared within the scope of a struct or class definition are a part of each instance of that type.

However, sometimes you may find that certain data or functions must be unique to the type in which they are declared, rather than to each instance of that type. It is for this purpose that the storage class attributes are provided, as discussed in the next section.

# Storage Classes

A storage class attribute is attached to variables to tell the compiler how data associated with that declaration should be stored. In essence, a storage class dictates a variable's lifetime with respect to its declaration scope. D provides two storage classes that affect a variable's lifetime: `auto` and `static`.

## Auto Storage Class

auto dictates that a variable's lifetime is tied to that of the enclosing scope. In other words, the memory reserved for auto variables is collected automatically when program execution leaves that scope. Here is an example:

```
import tango.io.Stdout;

int autoFunc( int x )
{
    auto int y;

    Stdout.formatln( "y is {}, setting to {}", y, x );
    y = x;
    return y;
```

```
}

void main()
{
    int ret;

    ret = autoFunc( 1 );
    Stdout.formatln( "autoFunc returned the value of y, which is set to {}", ret );
    ret = autoFunc( 2 );
    Stdout.formatln( "autoFunc returned the value of y, which is set to {}", ret );
}
```

Here, you can see that the value of y is not persistent across calls to autoFunc. Instead, space is allocated for y when autoFunc is called, and it is collected when autoFunc returns.

auto is the default storage class in D, so it is not necessary to precede variable declarations with auto. In practice, the most common use of an explicit auto storage class is for automatic type inference, as the presence of a storage class is necessary to indicate to the compiler that a statement is a declaration if the type qualifier is omitted.

## Static Storage Class

static dictates that a variable's lifetime is tied to that of the module in which it is declared. The variable is initialized once when the module is loaded, and it is available until the module is unloaded. Here is an example:

```
import tango.io.Stdout;

int staticFunc( int x )
{
    static int y;

    Stdout.formatln( "y is {}, setting to {}", y, x );
    y = x;
    return y;
}

void main()
{
    int ret;

    ret = staticFunc( 1 );
```

```
    Stdout.formatln( "autoFunc returned the value of y, which is set to {}", ret );
    ret = staticFunc( 2 );
    Stdout.formatln( "autoFunc returned the value of y, which is set to {}", ret );
}
```

Here, space is allocated for y when the module in which it is declared is loaded, and this space persists until the module is unloaded. Thus, the value of y is effectively persistent across calls to staticFunc. Static variables may be declared at any level and will behave the same way. However, static variables may be initialized only at the point of declaration if the initialization value can be computed at compile time. In other instances, a static constructor must be used, as explained next.

# Static Constructors

Attaching the static attribute to a constructor or destructor indicates that it should be associated with the lifetime of the enclosing module rather than with an instance of the enclosing type. In other words, static constructors are called when the module in which they are declared is loaded, and static destructors are called when the module is unloaded.

Static constructors are called in lexical order from the top to the bottom of the module, and static destructors are called in reverse lexical order. This order of processing guarantees that initialization dependencies are preserved within a module.

# Lifetime Characteristics of Modules

As you've learned in previous chapters, a D module is a file in which D code resides. Therefore, discussion of source files should be considered equivalent to discussion of modules. That said, it is preferable to think in terms of modules when evaluating program behavior because modules provide a means of encapsulation not unlike classes—they can contain constructors, destructors, and so on. With this in mind, a few issues must be considered with respect to procedural lifetime.

---

Note ➡ It is possible to subvert the one-file-per-module design through careful use of the module statement, but this is an advanced trick with few practical applications.

---

# Static Initialization Order

When a module is loaded, its static constructors will be called in lexical order from the top to the bottom of the file, regardless of their declaration scope. Thus, the following example should display ABC when run.

```
module MyModule;
import tango.io.Stdout;

struct MyStruct
{
    static this()
    {
        Stdout.formatln( "A" );
    }
}

static this()
{
    Stdout.formatln( "B" );
}

class MyClass
{
    static this()
    {
        Stdout.formatln( "C" );
    }
}

void main() {}
```

Similarly, to ensure that dependent variables are cleaned up in the proper order, a module's destructors will be called in reverse lexical order when the module is unloaded. Thus, the following example should display CBA when run:

```
module MyModule;
import tango.io.Stdout;

struct MyStruct
{
```

```
 static ~this()
    {
        Stdout.formatln( "A" );
    }
}

static ~this()
{
    Stdout.formatln( "B" );
}

class MyClass
{
    static ~this()
    {
        Stdout.formatln( "C" );
    }

}

void main() {}
```

## Module Initialization Order

While initialization within a module occurs relative to lexical order, an initialization order is defined only when importing two or more modules that have a dependency relationship and contain static constructors or destructors. For these sets of modules, their relative order of initialization is guaranteed to be performed relative to the dependencies defined by their import statements. For example, consider an application containing modules declared like so:

```
module E;
import tango.io.Stdout;

static this()
{
    Stdout.formatln( "E" );
}

module D;
```

```
import E;
import tango.io.Stdout;

static this()
{
    Stdout.formatln( "D" );
}

module C;
import tango.io.Stdout;

static this()
{
    Stdout.formatln( "C" );
}

module B;
import C;
import D;
import tango.io.Stdout;

static this()
{
    Stdout.formatln( "B" );
}

module A;
import C;
import tango.io.Stdout;

static this()
{
    Stdout.formatln( "A" );
}

module Main;
import A;
import B;
import tango.io.Stdout;

static this()
{
    Stdout.formatln( "Main" );
```

```
}

void main()
{
    Stdout.formatln( "Hello, World!" );
}
```

Displayed graphically, the modules exhibit the dependency relationships shown in Figure 4-1.

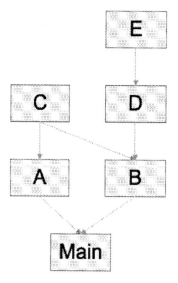

*Figure 4-1. Module dependency relationship in example of module initialization order*

Given this set of modules, it should be clear that Main depends on A and B, A depends on C, B depends on C and D, and D depends on E. Because all the involved modules contain static constructors, you can be sure that E will be initialized before D, which will in turn be initialized before B; that C will be initialized before both A and B; and that A and B will be initialized before Main. Running this program produces the following output:

```
C
A
E
D
B
Main
Hello, World!
```

However, other permutations are possible, as long as they maintain the dependency rules described earlier.

## Module Lifetime States

All modules statically reachable during compilation will be loaded on program initialization and unloaded on program termination. However, it may be useful to know the order in which each step involved in initialization and termination takes place "behind the scenes" in a D application.

Like an object, a D program has initialization, execution, and termination states. Also, if program initialization fails, the execution and termination states are never reached. However, if the program has been initialized successfully, its termination sequence will be run, even if execution completes via an unhandled exception. This mimics the behavior of an object as well, since scoped objects will have their destructor called on scope exit, regardless of whether scope is exited via a normal return or via a thrown exception.

The initialization process of a D program begins by loading and initializing all modules in the program according to the dependency rules described in the previous section. Once all modules have been loaded, any available unit tests will be executed. Then the program is considered to be in an initialized state, and execution begins.

Program execution continues until all non-daemon threads (including the main thread) have returned, either via normal processing or via an unhandled exception. Once this occurs, the program is considered to be in the termination (or halting) state.

---

Note ➡ A *non-daemon thread* is a thread whose isDaemon property is set to false. This value is false by default in Tango.

---

During program termination, all module destructors will be run according to the dependency rules outlined earlier, and then a normal garbage-collection cycle may occur to finalize any lingering objects. The program is then considered to have terminated, and any remaining resources will be unloaded as the process exits.

# Lifetime Characteristics of Functions

As you've learned, the static storage class is a means of extending the lifetime of data beyond that of the scope in which it is declared. But different types of non-static variables have varying lifetime characteristics when used as parameters to or return types of functions. The first of these are arrays.

## Lifetime of Arrays

As you learned in Chapter 2, D provides two kinds of arrays with similar semantics but distinct characteristics:

*Static array*: This type of array is called static because its size is fixed at compile time and may not change.

*Dynamic array*: This type of array is called dynamic because its size is not specified and therefore may be changed arbitrarily at runtime.

These two kinds of arrays exhibit the essential characteristics of a value and a reference type, respectively, but there are some subtle differences that should be noted.

---

Note ➡ Some languages use the terms *fixed-length arrays* and *variable-length arrays*. The terms *dynamic* and *static* are used here instead to be consistent with the D language specification. The term *static* here applies to whether the array may be resized, and has no relation to the static storage class in D.

---

### Static Arrays

Static arrays are value types, and as such, their footprint exists entirely at the point of declaration. If a static array is declared within a function call, its data will be rendered invalid when execution leaves the function, and declaring a static array within the body of a struct or class directly affects the memory required for an instance of that type. Static arrays are identified by a size qualifier in the appropriate dimension of an array declaration. Here is an example:

```
int[4]    varA;
int[2][4] varB;
```

In these declarations, varA is a static array that contains four int values, and varB is a two-dimensional static array that contains four static int arrays, each with room for two values. The memory reserved for static arrays matches exactly the size of the contained type multiplied by the number of elements in the array.

Unlike other value types, however, static arrays may not be used as return values for functions, and they are passed to functions by reference. Here is an example:

```
import tango.io.Stdout;

void alter( char[7] param )
{
    param[] = "7654321";
}

void main()
{
    char[7] message = "1234567";

    Stdout.formatln( "{}", message );
    alter( message );
    Stdout.formatln( "{}", message );
}
```

Because static arrays are value types, you might expect space to be reserved for param, and the current contents of message to be copied into this space when alter is called, thus localizing the operations performed on param to the scope of alter. This is not the case, however. All arrays—even static arrays—are actually passed by reference, and therefore the example prints "1234567" followed by "7654321."

In practice, the effect a length specifier has for array parameters is to restrict the type of data passed into the function and to dictate whether the array may be resized. It has no effect on whether that parameter is passed by value or by reference.

## Dynamic Arrays

The length of dynamic arrays is not fixed, and the memory to which a dynamic array refers may be shared with other dynamic arrays, it may reside on the stack, and so on.

Combined with the garbage-collection feature in D, dynamic arrays are often called *slices* to suggest that they may represent an arbitrary sequence, or slice, of data. In addition (and suggested by the *slice* terminology), dynamic arrays are not required to reference an entire array in order to preserve it from garbage collection. Such use of dynamic arrays lends a great deal of expressiveness to the language, and it can result in surprising performance gains by substantially reducing the number of memory allocations required for common operations.

Dynamic arrays are identified by the omission of a size qualifier in the appropriate dimension of an array declaration. Here is an example:

```
int[]    varA;
int[4][] varB;
```

In these declarations, varA is a dynamic array of int values, and varB is a dynamic array of static arrays, each containing a sequence of four int values. The memory reserved for dynamic arrays is equivalent to two pointer values from which the length of the array and a pointer to the array data may be obtained via the length and ptr properties, respectively.

As expected, dynamic arrays are passed by reference when used as function parameters. Dynamic arrays may be used as return values as well, and it is here that unexpected behavior may arise if you are not cautious. It was previously stated that dynamic arrays may refer to any sequence of memory. But what if that memory was not dynamically allocated? Consider the following example:

```
import tango.io.Stdout;

char[] getMessage()
{
    char[5] buf = "hello";
    char[]   ret = buf;

    return ret;
}

void main()
{
    char[] msg = getMessage();

    Stdout.formatln( "{}", msg );
}
```

When execution enters the getMessage function, space is reserved on the stack for buf, and the string "hello" is copied into that space. When buf is assigned to ret, however, ret merely obtains a reference to this data—no copying takes place. Thus, when execution leaves the scope of getMessage, the data space reserved for buf is collected, and the value portion of ret is copied and returned. Remember, however, that the value portion of a reference type is merely the reference itself, so msg is assigned a reference to data that no longer exists. The common term for such a variable is a *dangling reference*, and any use of msg prior to its reassignment to a valid data region will result in *undefined behavior*, which is essentially a technical term for "something bad" (usually data corruption or program failure).

## Lifetime of Delegates

Much as dynamic arrays may be used to reference data declared in an arbitrary scope, delegates may refer to functions declared in an arbitrary scope. And like dynamic arrays, data declared within a scope surrounding the referenced function may have a lifetime that is different from that of the reference itself.

---

Note ➡ References to functions declared at module scope are referred to as *function pointers*, and are represented by the `function` keyword. In the future, however, delegates will likely be able to refer to all function types.

---

Consider the `getMessage` example in the previous section. There, a reference to a function's local data was passed out of the scope in which that data was valid, causing unpredictable behavior if that reference were ever used. Delegates behave much the same way. Here is an example:

```
import tango.io.Stdout;

alias void delegate() Operation;

void perform( Operation op )
{
    op();
}

Operation func()
{
    int x = 0;

    void putAndIncrement()
    {
        Stdout.formatln( "x is {}", x++ );
    }
```

```
        perform( &putAndIncrement );
        return &putAndIncrement;
}

void main()
{
        Operation op = func();
        perform( op );
}
```

In this program, the function putAndIncrement is declared within the scope of func and therefore has access to the variables declared within func, as well as to those in surrounding scopes. This is fine for the call to perform that occurs within the scope of func, because execution has not yet left the scope of func, and therefore any data it contains is valid. So, the first call to perform should print x is 0 to the console. But then a reference to putAndIncrement is returned as a delegate, and execution leaves the scope of func, causing the data it contains to be collected. At this point, any further reference to x invokes undefined behavior.

---

Note ➡ A recent addition to D 2.0 provides experimental support for full closures. This should eliminate all the issues described here by dynamically generating a copy of the referenced calling context if needed.

---

One important issue to be aware of is that delegates do not reference variable data directly, but rather reference the *calling context* in which these variables are declared. So the problem with putAndIncrement was not that x is a value type so much as that the calling context no longer exists. Consider the following program, which substitutes a reference type for x:

```
import tango.io.Stdout;

alias void delegate() Operation;

void perform( Operation op )
{
        op();
}

Operation func()
{
        char[] message = "hello";
```

```
    void putMessage()
    {
        Stdout.formatln( message );
    }

    perform( &putMessage );
    return &putMessage;
}

void main()
{
    Operation op = func();
    perform( op );
}
```

This program will print `hello` to the console, as expected, and then enter the realm of undefined behavior, just like the previous program. To help clarify why this is so, assume that a calling context is something like a struct, and it is this to which the delegate refers. So when `func` returns, the context struct is collected, and the delegate no longer has any way to reference data local to `func`.

## Lazy Expressions

*Lazy expressions* are a convenience type for delaying the evaluation of an expression used as a function parameter. Their primary advantage over the use of delegate literals is that the user of a function with lazy arguments doesn't need to be aware that some of the parameters may not be evaluated immediately, while the use of delegate literals makes this explicit.

It is important to note that lazy expressions are merely a convenient method for working with a specific kind of delegate, and they are represented as delegates internally by the compiler. For this reason, the behavior of lazy expressions should be considered identical to that of delegates in the same context. Fortunately, lazy expressions are not implicitly convertible to delegates, so it is difficult to use them in a dangerous manner.

# Garbage Collection

By default, dynamic memory allocations performed in D via `new`, by manipulation of the `length` property for arrays, and by array operations such as concatenation and appending of elements are provided by a garbage-collecting allocator. D imposes no functional requirements on the actual garbage-collector implementation, but typically, a garbage collector will periodically identify memory blocks that are no longer referenced by the application, finalize these blocks if appropriate for the data they contained, and then reuse the freed memory for future allocations.

Concerning the lifetime of types, the important issue is that the collection of a given memory block is not guaranteed to occur in a timely manner, and some blocks may be missed entirely. While this may be an unnecessarily grim proclamation concerning the reliability of automatic garbage collection, it is an important issue to be aware of in times where the observable lifetime of data is important. In practice, the safest approach is to avoid reliance on a destructor to clean up limited resources unless the object's lifetime is explicitly managed either manually or via the scope attribute.

As one basic example, consider an object that represents a file:

```
class File
{
    this( char[] name )
    {
        fd = open( name );
    }

    ~this()
    {
        close( fd );
    }

    private int fd;
}
```

Further, assume that the operating system on which this program runs allows a process to maintain a maximum of ten open files at a time. If a program operates on a large number of individual files and simply discards the objects when done (instead of destroying them explicitly with delete), it is conceivable that the program could reach a state where no more file descriptors are available and yet the garbage collector has not yet collected any file objects, even though some may be available for collection.

In short, it is not safe to assume that the garbage collector knows more about what needs to be done than you do yourself. If any object owns a limited resource, consider managing its lifetime explicitly rather than relying on the garbage collector to take care of things in a timely manner. It is also a good habit to get used to D's scope attribute (discussed in Chapter 3) and scope statement (discussed in Chapter 2) to simplify the management of such objects. By doing so, your applications will be more reliable and more efficient.

This completes our discussion of the lifetimes associated with the different D types. Understanding the language's behavior is this regard will help you to avoid many problems. In the next chapter, you'll learn about D's templates, which are powerful programming tools.

# CHAPTER 5

# Templates

Like many modern programming languages, D supports the use of generic programming to simplify coding. This is done using templates, and as you'll learn in this chapter, both type and function templates are supported. Additionally, this chapter covers template specialization, template metaprogramming, and compile-time function evaluation.

## The Problem of Insufficient Information

In a statically typed language like D, object-oriented programming is a means of abstraction based on certain predefined characteristics. As you learned in Chapter 3, a set of characteristics common to a particular concept are specified in an interface, and a function written to operate on an interface is then able to manipulate any number of different objects as long as they implement that interface. Thus, the efficacy of object-oriented programming is related to its ability to ignore all the details about a type except some aspect relevant to the task at hand. However, problems arise when the information common to a collection of types is not sufficient for the operations to be performed on those types.

For example, consider the implementation of a simple data structure such as a linked list. To eliminate code duplication, a single implementation of such a container should be able to hold every type used in the program. The natural solution is to design the container to operate in terms of some common interface:

```
module ObjectList;

class List
{
    void insert( Object o )
    {
        head = new Node( o, head );
    }

    int opApply( int delegate( inout Object ) dg )
    {
        for( Node n = head; n; n = n.next )
```

```
        {
            if( auto r = dg( n.elem ) )
                return r;
        }
        return 0;
    }
private:
    static class Node
    {
        Object elem;
        Node    next;

        this( Object e, Node n )
        {
            elem = e;
            next = n;
        }
    }

    Node head;
}
```

In this case, the list is implemented in terms of the interface common to all class types: Object. Thus, any class instance may be inserted into the list, and the list provides a means of observing its contents using a foreach statement:

```
import ObjectList;
import tango.io.Stdout;

void main()
{
    class Integer
    {
        int val;

        this( int v )
        {
            val = v;
        }
    }

    auto list = new List;
```

```
    for( int i = 3; i; --i )
        list.insert( new Integer( i ) );

    foreach( elem; list )
        Stdout.formatln( "{}", (cast(Integer) elem).val );
}
```

Notice that in this program, too little information has been preserved regarding the data stored within list. This is evident because of the cast operation needed to operate on that data. Here, program integrity relies on the programmer's knowledge that list will contain only instances of Integer. Furthermore, if something other than an Integer is inserted into list, the print routine must signal a runtime error to address the problem. In light of this issue, the attempt to eliminate one problem—the need to maintain duplicate specialized linked lists—has been replaced with another: reduced compile-time checking of program integrity. A more desirable solution is some means of eliminating the need to maintain duplicate code without sacrificing the compile-time checking that accompanies such a design. This is the solution available through the use of templates.

# Type Templates

*Templates* are a means of performing compile-time code generation using a structured form of symbol replacement. In essence, templates recruit the compiler to generate the type-specific versions of generic code that you would otherwise need to maintain manually. In D, templates are specified using the following syntax:

```
template MyTemplate( T )
{

}
```

Such a template block effectively introduces a new namespace and may contain any code that would be valid within the top-level module namespace, such as variable declarations and class and function definitions. This particular template introduces the symbol MyTemplate into the top-level symbol table of the module in which it is declared, and accepts one template parameter: T. This syntax requires T to be a valid type name, and the compiler will replace every instance of T within the template block with the type name supplied by the user.

Templates are instantiated by specifying their parameters in parentheses, prefixed by an exclamation mark. So an instance of MyTemplate with T expanded as int would be MyTemplate!(int). By itself, this is not a valid expression; it is merely a partial symbol name that will effectively be used as a prefix for all symbol names contained within the template block.

Now, let's rewrite the linked-list implementation shown in the preceding section as a template. In this case, we want the template block to contain one thing: the definition of the List class. And the class should work for any supplied type T in place of an Object base type. By enclosing the class declaration in a template block and replacing the word Object with a template type parameter name (we will use T), we have the following code:

```
module TemplateList;

template List( T )
{
    class List
    {
        void insert( T val )
        {
            head = new Node( val, head );
        }

        int opApply( int delegate( inout T ) dg )
        {
            for( Node n = head; n; n = n.next )
            {
                if( auto r = dg( n.elem ) )
                    return r;
            }
            return 0;
        }

    private:
        static class Node
        {
            T       elem;
            Node    next;

            this( T e, Node n )
            {
                elem = e;
                next = n;
            }
        }

        Node head;
```

```
    }
}
```

To create an instance of this `List` class, the basic format is as described earlier: `List!(int).List` is the full type specification of a `List` specialized for the element type `int`. But notice the redundancy within the symbol name. If a template block contains only one symbol and that symbol has the same name as the template itself, D allows the redundant portion of the declaration to be omitted. Thus, the declaration `List!(int).List` can be shortened to `List!(int)`. Similarly, if a template block contains only one symbol and that symbol introduces its own scope (that is, if it is a class, struct, or function definition), then D allows the template block to be omitted by transferring the template parameter list to immediately after the symbol name. Thus, the preceding template class could be rewritten like this:

```
class List( T )
{
    void insert( T val )
    {
        head = new Node( val, head );
    }

    // And so on
}
```

Notice also that instead of working exclusively with objects, templates can be defined for any valid type. So the first programming example can be rewritten as follows:

```
import TemplateList;
import tango.io.Stdout;

void main()
{
    auto list = new List!(int);
    for( int i = 3; i; --i )
        list.insert( i );

    foreach( elem; list )
        Stdout.formatln( "{}", elem );
}
```

Although maintaining collections of objects is an important part of any program, the feature is largely useless without some means of operating on the contained data. Functions provide a way to perform such operations.

# Function Templates

Based on the sample program in the previous section, let's assume that one desired feature is a means of printing the contents of a container. Rather than writing the code explicitly every time we want to perform this action, it would be preferable to place it in a function somewhere. One option would be to add a `printContents()` routine to every container. However, this once again introduces needless code duplication for an operation that is essentially the same regardless of the container type. In fact, given the iteration concept employed by `foreach`, the only portion that will change in this case is the type of the element and the container. Fortunately, templates may be applied to functions as well as classes, with essentially the same syntax:

```
import TemplateList;
import tango.io.Stdout;

void printContents( T )( T list )
{
    foreach( elem; list )
        Stdout.formatln( "{}", elem );
}

void main()
{
    auto list = new List!(int);

    for( int i = 3; i; --i )
        list.insert( i );

    printContents!(List!(int))( list );
}
```

Obviously, this calling syntax leaves a lot to be desired, as it is complicated even for this relatively simple case. For this reason, D allows template type parameters to be omitted as long as they can be inferred from the function arguments. And if no template parameters are required, the template portion of the statement can be omitted entirely. This is the case with the call to `printContents` in the example, so we can rewrite the call as `printContents( list )`.

Like normal functions, template functions may be overloaded by one another. However, remember that the declaration `printContents( T )( T val )` is actually an abbreviated syntax for the following:

```
template printContents( T )
{
    void printContents( T val )
    {

    }
}
```

This is important because template functions in D are actually just functions inside a template block. In other words, the symbol exposed to the surrounding namespace is the name of the template, not the name of the function. In effect, to overload a template function, the template symbol name and parameter set must collectively be unique for the scope in which the template is declared. Thus, to declare an overload for printContents that accepts dynamic arrays containing elements of any type, we must add a second "dummy" template parameter to avoid a conflict with the other printContents template function in the same namespace:

```
void printContents( T, U = void )( T[] list )
{
    Stdout.formatln( "{} elements:", list.length );
    foreach( elem; list )
        Stdout.formatln( "{}", elem );
}
```

Notice that this also demonstrates that template parameters may be supplied with default values. Unlike default values for function parameters, however, defaults may be supplied for any parameter, regardless of position. So the previous function could be rewritten like this:

```
void printContents( U = void, T )( T[] list )
{

}
```

More important, however, is that template type parameters may be used to represent only a portion of an actual type. In this case, for example, T represents only the element portion of the dynamic array type declaration. When multiple function templates are valid overloads for a given function call, the compiler will choose the most *specialized* function; that is, the compiler will choose the function for which T represents the smallest portion of the function parameters. This can be most easily illustrated with an example:

```
void func( T )( T val )
{
    pragma( msg, "func( T )( T val )" );
```

```
}

void func(T, U = void )( T[] val )
{
    pragma( msg, "func( T )( T[] val )" );
}

void func( T, U = void, V = void )( T* val )
{
    pragma( msg, "func( T )( T* val )" );
}

void main()
{
    int    i;
    int*   p;
    int[]  a;

    func( i );
    func( p );
    func( a );
}
```

Here, func( i ) should choose the first routine, func( p ) should choose the second, and func( a ) should choose the third. And T will be expanded as int in all three cases.

---

Note ➡ Although the reduced syntax of the printContents function call looks identical to that of a normal function call, D 1.0 does not allow template functions to be overloaded with nontemplate functions. Support for overloading template functions with normal functions will be added in D 2.0.

---

# Template Specialization

Although we said that template symbol names are required to be unique within their enclosing scope, this is not strictly true. Templates may have the same name and set of parameters as long as, beyond the generic case, specializations are provided for those templates to distinguish the choice between templates for any set of template parameters.

The form for supplying a template parameter specialization is T : S, where T is a template parameter and S is a subclass of the symbols to which T may apply. For example, the templates in the following set do not conflict because they are specialized for different types:

```
template List( T )
{
    pragma( msg, "List( T )" );
}

template List( T : int )
{
    pragma( msg, "List( T : int )" );
}

template List( T : T[] )
{
    pragma( msg, "List( T : T[] )" );
}

void main()
{
    alias List!(char)   A;
    alias List!(int)    B;
    alias List!(char[]) C;
}
```

In this example, the most general, or default, template List( T ) is chosen for the instantiation List!(char) because there is no appropriate match among the specializations. The remaining two instantiations have matching specializations, however, so the compiler chooses them instead.

Note that this specialization mechanism works only when the template parameters are explicitly specified rather than inferred as a part of a function template call. Therefore, such specializations are typically more appropriate for type templates than for function templates.

# Template Metaprogramming

*Template metaprogramming* traditionally describes the use of templates to perform tasks for which they were not originally designed. The practice of metaprogramming relies on the knowledge that templates provide a means for looping, Boolean logic, and so on, and are therefore a logically complete language in and of themselves. In D, compile-time function evaluation (discussed at the end of this chapter) has rendered many of the traditional uses for template metaprogramming obsolete, but this approach warrants some discussion, simply to introduce the sort of advanced features and techniques available to the discerning metaprogrammer.

# Template Value Parameters

The first and most common tool for template metaprogramming is the use of value parameters in template blocks. Previously, we explored the use of types as template parameters, but many primitive value types may be used as template parameters as well. The same basic rules for overloading and symbol collision apply, only in this case, we are comparing values instead of types. Here's an example:

```
enum Color
{
    RED,
    BLUE
}

template Choice( int i : 1 )
{
    pragma( msg, "Choice: int = 1" );
}

template Choice( int i : 2 )
{
    pragma( msg, "Choice: int = 2" );
}

template Choice( bool b : true )
{
    pragma( msg, "Choice: bool = true" );
}

template Choice( float f )
{
    pragma( msg, "Choice: float = ?" );
}

template Choice( Color c : Color.BLUE )
{
```

```
        pragma( msg, "Choice: Color = BLUE" );
}

template Choice( char[] s )
{
        pragma( msg, "Choice: s = " ~ s );
}

void main()
{
        alias Choice!(1)    A;
        alias Choice!(2)    B;
        alias Choice!(3.0)  C;
        alias Choice!(true) D;
        alias Choice!(Color.BLUE)  E;
        alias Choice!("Hello, D!") F;
}
```

Template value parameters may also be freely combined with template type parameters, or expanded based on a supplied type parameter:

```
template Choice( T, size_t size : 4 = T.sizeof )
{
        pragma( msg, "Choice: size = 4" );
}

template Choice( T, size_t size : 8 = T.sizeof )
{
        pragma( msg, "Choice: size = 8" );
}

void main()
{
        alias Choice!(int)  A;
        alias Choice!(long) B;
}
```

Here, we have a template with a type parameter and a specialized value parameter, which has a default that depends on the type parameter. When int is passed as the type for T, size is initialized by default to int.sizeof, or 4. The compiler then chooses the appropriate specialization for the template signature Choice!(int,4), which is the first of the two supplied templates in the sample code.

It should be evident that template specializations can quickly become quite complex, particularly using dependent value parameters, but the basic rule is fairly simple: pick all templates with the appropriate number and order of types and values, expand any default parameters, and then choose the specialization that most closely fits this expanded parameter list. If there is a conflict, a compilation error will occur.

# Boolean Logic

Boolean logic is simply a choice between a set of options based on the evaluation of an expression. In D, this logic is typically performed using if/else and switch statements, but similar behavior can be performed at compile time using template specializations.

## if/else Templates

Performing if/else logic in templates is a matter of providing two specializations for Boolean parameter values of true and false, and relying on compile-time optimizations (constant folding) to evaluate the expression on which the choice is based. In metaprogramming, it is most common for this expression to exist in yet another template that evaluates to a Boolean value. For example, let's assume that we want to declare a different type based on the size of a supplied type. The following is a fairly traditional means of performing this in template language:

```
import tango.io.Stdout;

template ChooseType( bool b )
{
    alias long ChooseType;
}

template ChooseType( bool b : true )
{
    alias short ChooseType;
}

template isSizeLessThan4( T )
{
    const bool isSizeLessThan4 = T.sizeof < 4;
}

void main()
```

```
{
    alias ChooseType!(isSizeLessThan4!(int))  WhenGreaterThan4;
    alias ChooseType!(isSizeLessThan4!(byte)) WhenLessThan4;

    Stdout.formatln( "WhenGreaterThan4.sizeof = {}", WhenGreaterThan4.sizeof );
    Stdout.formatln( "WhenLessThan4.sizeof = {}", WhenLessThan4.sizeof );
}
```

Here, our if/else logic resides in the ChooseType template. The initial block without a specialization condition is the default, and the second block is specialized for conditions where the supplied template parameter evaluates to true. Thus, the second block represents an if condition, and the first represents an else condition. The expression here is encapsulated in another template, named appropriately isSizeLessThan4. Thus, given the alias declarations in main, we should expect isSizeLessThan4 in the first alias, WhenGreaterThan4, to evaluate to false and therefore select the default ChooseType template, making WhenGreaterThan4 an alias for long. Similarly, isSizeLessThan4 evaluates to true in the second alias, thus making WhenLessThan4 an alias for short.

## static if Statements

The preceding section was a taste of traditional template metaprogramming, and should be sufficient to demonstrate both the power and the complexity of such code. Fortunately, such code is extremely rare in D, because it provides much simpler and more powerful tools to solve the same problems. The most common of these is the static if statement, which works exactly like a normal if statement, but at compile time. Also, static if statements may be used in any scope and do not introduce a scope of their own.

In the previous example, a static if statement allows the specializations of ChooseType to be collapsed into a single template block, which is much more readable than the prior implementation:

```
template ChooseType( bool b )
{
    static if( b )
        alias short ChooseType;
    else
        alias long ChooseType;
}
```

## is Expressions

The is expression is a compile-time feature that eliminates the need for nearly all of the complex machinery traditionally required to determine information about a type. The most common forms of the is expression are the following:

```
is( Type )                          // A
is( Type : TypeSpecialization )   // B
is( Type == TypeSpecialization ) // C
```

The form labeled A evaluates to true if Type is semantically correct. Thus, the following template tests whether the supplied type is a pointer by attempting to dereference it:

```
import tango.io.Stdout;

template isPointer( T )
{
    const bool isPointer = is( typeof(*T) );
}

void main()
{
    Stdout.formatln( "isPointer!(int) = {}", isPointer!(int) );
    Stdout.formatln( "isPointer!(char*) = {}", isPointer!(char*) );
}
```

Perhaps more common are the forms labeled B and C, which test whether Type is convertible to TypeSpecialization and whether Type is an exact match of TypeSpecialization. Here is an example:

```
import tango.io.Stdout;

template convertsToAnInt( T )
{
    const bool convertsToAnInt = is( T : int );
}

template isExactlyAnInt( T )
{
    const bool isExactlyAnInt = is( T == int );
}

void main()
{
```

```
    Stdout.formatln( "convertsToAnInt!(byte) = {}", convertsToAnInt!(byte) );
    Stdout.formatln( "convertsToAnInt!(char*) = {}", convertsToAnInt!(char*) );
    Stdout.formatln( "isExactlyAnInt!(int) = {}", isExactlyAnInt!(int) );
    Stdout.formatln( "isExactlyAnInt!(byte) = {}", isExactlyAnInt!(byte) );
}
```

This code should print the following output:

```
convertsToAnInt!(byte) = true
convertsToAnInt!(char*) = false
isExactlyAnInt!(int) = true
isExactlyAnInt!(byte) = false
```

Finally, form C also allows the category of a type to be determined by supplying one of the following type categories in place of a TypeSpecialization: typedef, struct, union, class, interface, enum, function, delegate, or super.


# Looping

To return to traditional means of template metaprogramming for a moment, it may be useful to know how looping can be performed with template expansion. Like if/else templates, value parameter specializations are employed to perform the loop body and to trap the termination condition. This is done via recursive template expansion:

```
template WhileNotZero( int i )
{
    pragma( msg, "Hello, D!" );
    alias WhileNotZero!(i - 1) Dummy;
}

template WhileNotZero( int i : 0 )
{
    // Terminate loop
}

void main()
{
    alias WhileNotZero!(3) LoopThreeTimes;
}
```

Here, the template WhileNotZero will initially be instantiated with i equal to 3, and it will, in turn, instantiate another version of WhileNotZero with i = i - 1. With i being decremented once for each instantiation of WhileNotZero, the specialization for i : 0 should be reached after three such expansions, at which time the template will be fully instantiated and compilation will continue.

---

Note ➡ A feature intended for inclusion in D 2.0 is support for static foreach. This should effectively eliminate the need for traditional template looping as described in this section.

---

# Compile-Time Function Evaluation

Perhaps the most useful tool available for metaprogramming in D is compile-time function evaluation (CTFE). This involves normal functions which, because everything they depend on is known at compile time, may be evaluated by the compiler at compile time when their result is assigned to a compile-time value.

Because the CTFE syntax is the same as normal runtime functions—and, in fact, the same code may be used in either case based on where the call is made—a simple demonstration of this feature should be sufficient to show its power:

```
import tango.io.Stdout;

int multiply( int x, int y )
{
    int result = 0;
    for( int i = 0; i < y; ++i )
        result += x;
    return result;
}

void main()
{
    static const result = multiply( 2, 3 );
    Stdout.formatln( "2 * 3 is {}", result );
}
```

The important issue to note here is that because result must be initialized at compile time, multiply is evaluated at compile time to do so. If for some reason multiply cannot be evaluated at compile time, such as if it performs input/output, dynamic memory allocation, or the like, then a compilation error will be generated for its use as a compile-time function.

Because of the relative simplicity of compile-time functions compared to those created with template metaprogramming, CTFE should be the preferred method for writing compile-time code. However, each technique has different strengths, and you are likely to encounter both in D programs, so it is useful to understand the fundamentals of both approaches.

The next chapter discusses Tango's text-processing functions.

# CHAPTER 6

# Text Processing

Text processing is, together with mathematics, the most important basic discipline in programming. Almost all data produced by humans will, at some point, be represented as text, or strings, in your system.

As you learned in Chapter 2, D provides basic string types, making the definition and usage of strings a breeze. An additional feature of strings is that they already are encoded as 8-, 16-, or 32-bit Unicode. This means that you can use D immediately in internationalized environments. You also can manipulate the encoding of strings directly.

Considering that Tango is a general-purpose library, text processing is given a prominent place via the tango.text package, and this chapter will cover most of the important functionality available there.

In this chapter, we'll begin by discussing the basic string-manipulation utilities present in Tango. Then we'll describe the Text class that Tango provides as a string wrapper; discuss conversions between strings, numeric types, and dates and times; and finally, explain how to do text formatting using Tango's Layout class.

## String-Manipulation Utilities

The string-manipulation utilities in Tango are functions that perform common operations on strings. You will find all of the basic string operation utilities in tango.text.Util. Other modules contain more advanced functionality, such as regular-expression handling and encoding-specific operations. This section focuses on the operations in the Util module and the tango.text.stream package.

---

Tip ➡ tango.core.Array contains generalized operations for arrays of all types, not only strings.

---

All of the functionality in tango.text.Util is presented through function templates that can be instantiated implicitly and called in the same manner as any other free functions. They can generally be divided into three main groups of functionality:

- Functions that can be used to modify a string's content in various ways

- Functions that help you search text

- Functions that lets you split a string into several components, especially for iteration

Let's explore each of these groups, further subdividing the third into splitting strings and splitting streams.

## MEMORY ALLOCATION AND TEXT-PROCESSING OPERATIONS

Throughout Tango, an effort is made to minimize memory allocation when performing operations. This is particularly apparent in the text-processing APIs. The various functions never allocate memory unless it is strictly necessary; in which case, it is a fallback solution.

You can allocate memory yourself if required, and pass it along to the operations you are going to use. In the following example, src is a list of strings to append with a comma in between, and buffer is a block of user-allocated memory. If buffer is too small, the result will be put on the heap instead.

```
char[15] buffer;
auto result = join(src, ",", buffer);
```

If speed or memory usage is of no importance to you, some of the most common operations have allocating wrappers for more immediate usage.

## String-Modifying Operations

The trim and strip functions are mainly used to clean up strings that may be padded at the start or the end, either with whitespace or other characters.

trim is the simplest operation, removing whitespace from the beginning and end of the input text, so that you're left with the content only. The returned string is a slice of your original, so you will need to duplicate it if you want to manipulate it further.

strip is a generalized version of trim, where you can pass it any character that should be removed from either end of the input string. As with trim, a clean slice of the original argument is returned.

Several functions let you edit the content itself. replace and substitute both replace occurrences of a specified pattern with a different one. replace replaces single characters with a new character. substitute replaces a substring of the input with a new string. Both of these operations do the replacement in place to avoid allocations. If you want to keep the original, duplicate it before passing it to either of these functions, as in the following example:

```
char[] original = "A string to have some letters replaced";
auto result = replace (original.dup, 'r' , 'l');
```

The end result of this example is the string "A stling to have some lettels leplaced."

The utilities include two simple operations to build strings: join and repeat. join concatenates a list of strings into a single big one. An optional postfix can be passed to the function that will be appended to each of the joined strings except the last. If you want to control the output buffer, you can pass your own to the function. repeat builds a string by repeating a pattern *n* times. This function also accepts an optional output buffer.

## String-Searching Operations

The next set of operations provides querying capabilities to help you find the location of certain substrings or to determine whether they are present.

contains and containsPattern check an input string for an embedded character or string, respectively. They both will return true if a match is found.

locate, locatePrior, locatePattern, and locatePatternPrior operate in a similar manner, except that they return the position in the input string of the first match. The first two look for a character. locate searches from the start of the string or starts at the optional start parameter. locatePrior starts at the end going toward the beginning or starts at the optional starting position. locatePattern and locatePatternPrior do the same, but they look for substrings (patterns) instead. In the case that no match is found, the length of the source string is returned instead. Here is an example:

```
locatePatternPrior ("ababababaaaab", "aba", 8);
```

This example returns 6 as the first position where the pattern aba starts, going backward from index 8.

---

Note ➡ Typically, most libraries return -1 when a pattern has not been found. That Tango does not do this means that the result in all cases can be used as a valid index into a slice.

---

If you need to check if a given character is whitespace, pass it to `isSpace`, which will return `true` if it is.

`matching`, `indexOf`, and `mismatch` provide highly efficient routines that you can use for testing certain aspects of your strings. `matching` returns `true` if both of the strings are equal up to the specified length. `indexOf` returns the index of the first match up to the specified length. In the case where no match is found, this length is returned. The returned index itself is zero-based. `mismatch` does the opposite, returning the first index where the strings no longer match. If the strings are actually matching, the length is returned instead.

## String-Splitting Operations

In the cases where you need to separate strings on a given pattern, several approaches are available through Tango. The first approach uses the operation `delimit`, `split`, or `splitLines`, returning an array of strings. `delimit` takes an array of delimiting characters, each of which results in a new string being put into the result array where one of those delimiters is found in the source string. `split` does the same thing, except that it looks for one given pattern. `splitLines` returns an array of distinct lines (as given by the presence of \n or \r\n in the source string). All of these functions remove from the resulting arrays the characters or patterns used.

If you prefer to iterate over the resulting components instead of receiving an array of them, `tango.text.Util` provides some efficient alternatives, using slices to make sure no allocations are made during the split operation itself. `lines`, `delimiters`, `patterns`, and `quotes` are all entities that can be used in `foreach`. Here is an example:

```
foreach (segment; patterns("one, two, three", ", ")) {
    . . .
}
```

This example will loop on each segment found in the string passed—in this case, one, two, and three.

If you would rather replace the delimiting pattern with a new one, the new pattern can be passed as an additional string to `patterns`. `lines` will let you iterate over the lines in your string, similar to `splitLines`. `delimiters` is the iterator version of `delimit`, whereas `quotes` will ignore delimiters found inside a pair of quotation marks, such as in the following example:

```
foreach (segment, quotes ("one two 'three four' five", " ")) {
    . . .
}
```

The results of this example are the segments one, two, three four, and five.

## Stream-Splitting Operations

In Tango, you will also find proper support for splitting operations over streams, whether you stream data from a file, a socket, a pipe, or any other class implementing the InputStream interface (see Chapter 7). Four stream iterators are available, all based on the StreamIterator superclass, and you can further extend this number by creating other subclasses. The iterators can all be found in the tango.text.stream package.

The following example demonstrates iterating over the elements of a stream:

```
import tango.io.FileConduit,
       tango.io.Console;
import tango.text.stream.LineIterator;

foreach (line; new LineIterator!(char) ( new FileConduit ("filename") ))
    Cout (line).newline;
```

This example uses the LineIterator on a stream from a file. The iterators are templated for each of the three character types in D. In this example, char is used. Each line is simply output to the console.

The other iterators are SimpleIterator, which takes a delimiter parameter in addition to the stream; QuoteIterator, which ignores delimiters within quotation marks; and RegexIterator, which lets you specify a regular expression to use as the delimiting pattern.

---

Note ➡ *Regular expressions* are patterns that usually are more complex than those that match a literal string. Regular expressions can be considered a language of their own.

---

# Text Class

Tango's Text class is in tango.text.Text. This class wraps a string array for you, keeps a current selection of where you last interacted with the string, and ensures proper and efficient operation.

The Text class provides for an object-oriented approach to the most common functionality in the basic text-processing routines. It abstracts away the potentially complex parts of string manipulation, especially where there may be a danger of slicing into the middle of Unicode code units.

When instantiating Text, the char type is used if the string needs to be specified. Text also implements the interface TextView, which can be used as a read-only gateway to the string. TextView's superinterface is UniText, which enables conversion of the string to one of the other Unicode encodings.

The main means of operating on the string wrapped by Text is to select a portion of it and then perform an operation on that selection.

## Read-Only View Methods

The methods in the read-only view of Text mainly let you query the text for various information and compare it to other instances, whether they are of the TextView type or a D string type.

The length of the text, a hash of it, and the encoding (represented as a TypeInfo instance) are available through the properties length, toHash, and encoding.

Both opCmp and opEquals are overloaded, as is the duplicate functionality also available through the methods compare and equals. In addition, you can check whether your text starts with or ends with a given substring.

The other methods of the read-only view are slice, copy, and comparator. If you use slice, you get the underlying array as a slice. The array is not in itself safe, as there is no way in D 1.0 to restrict its use, and so you are expected to respect that it should not be changed through this interface.

With comparator, you can set the algorithms that are used in different comparison methods, and copy accepts a target array into which you can copy the text's content.

## Modifying Methods

After instantiating Text, either with or without content, the content can be set/reset using two set methods. One takes a D string of the type that the instance was created with, and the other takes a TextView instance. Both have an optional parameter that can be set to false if the instance is not intended for modification of the contents.

Almost all of the methods in Text return an instance of the enclosing class, making it possible to chain calls, as in this example:

```
auto text = new Text!(char)("The couple danced the rumba");
text.select("couple");
text.replace("party").prepend("large ").select("rumba");
text.replace("tango");
```

This sequence results in the content "The large party danced the tango."

## Selecting a Part of the Text

Since selecting a portion of the text to operate on is important, the Text class provides several ways to do this. To select a part of the text, you can use either an explicit or implicit approach.

select(int, int) allows you to perform an explicit selection, as you can set the start and end index of your selection.

To perform an implicit selection, you pass a character, a pattern (D string), or a TextView instance to select or selectPrior. These will search for the given argument, either toward the end or toward the front from the current selection, and set the selection to the match. If the argument wasn't found, the method you called will return false.

When you need to see what is selected, you can obtain the selected slice via the selection property. You can also get the starting index and length by calling selectionSpan.

## Operating on a Selection

Most of the modifying methods of Text operate based on the current selection. By using append, you can append some text directly to the current selection. This text can be a character (or the same character multiple times), a D string, a TextView instance, or a number. The append methods that accept numeric arguments can take additional formatting hints. If you need to append text that is not in the same Unicode encoding as your text, append and transcode it by using the encode method.

Similar to append, prepend allows you to put some text immediately ahead of the current selection.

A selection can also be replaced by a string by using replace with the string you want to use as the replacement. To completely remove a selection, use remove. You can also truncate the text, in which case the default behavior is to truncate at the end of the current selection.

## Performing Nonselection Operations

A few operations operate independently of the selection. clear empties the content completely, and reserve lets you reserve space for coming insertions and additions. trim and strip operate in the same way as the corresponding functions in tango.text.Util.

# Text Combined with the Utilities

For additional power, Text can be combined with the utilities in tango.text.Util, as in the following example, where the line iterator is used to iterate over lines in a Text instance.

```
auto source = new Text!(char)("one\ntwo\nthree");

foreach (line; Util.lines(source.slice)) {
    . . .
}
```

Similarly, all instances of a word in a block of text can be replaced with another:

```
auto dst = new Text!(char);
foreach (element; Util.patterns ("all cows eat grass", "eat", "chew")) {
    dst.append (element);
}
```

# Numeric Conversion

An important facet of text processing is the conversion of text to and from different representation, such as numeric values. Tango has a full set of operations to efficiently convert from text into the various numeric types in the language, as well as support for parsing date and time information.

Tango provides this conversion through three modules—tango.text.convert.Integer, Float, and TimeStamp—and makes sure that the conversion can be done without any heap activity unless strictly necessary for other reasons.

Each of these modules has two common operations that function as the main workhorses of the converters: parse to convert from a text to some numeric type, and format to convert from a number into a textual representation. These give you full control of the process.

# Formatting a Value into a String

Following the Tango convention, `format` requires that you pass along an output buffer for the result. Here is an example where the number 15 is formatted:

```
char[10] output;
auto result = format (output, 15);
```

In this example, the formatted number is placed into `output`, which, in this case, is allocated on the stack. The result returned is a slice of `output` containing the exact string. Many of the `format` functions provide additional parameters so you can better control the formatted output.

# Converting Strings into Numeric Types

Creating a value in a numeric type based on a textual representation is the opposite operation to formatting. `parse` supports additional parameters to control the output, such as to say something about the radix used.

# Converting Integers

The `Integer` module lets you convert to or from the types `short`, `ushort`, `int`, `uint`, `long`, and `ulong`. In this module, `parse` can take three arguments:

- The first argument is the string to be parsed,

- The second argument can be a `uint` describing the radix. If omitted, `10` is the default.

- As a third argument, you can pass a pointer to a `uint`, which will be set to a number representing how much of the string was processed to create the result.

In the same vein, `format` has two additional parameters with default values. The first two are always the output buffer and the number to be formatted. The third is a style identifier that says how the number is to be represented in the resulting text. You can choose from the values shown in Table 6-1.

*Table 6-1. Style Identifiers Available for Integer.parse*

| Style Identifier | Description |
| --- | --- |
| Style.Unsigned | Format as unsigned decimal |
| Style.Signed | Format as signed decimal (the default) |
| Style.Octal | Format as an octal number |
| Style.Hex | Format as a lowercase hexadecimal number |
| Style.HexUpper | Format as an uppercase hexadecimal number |
| Style.Binary | Format as a binary number |

In addition to specifying how the number should be formatted, you can pass along a style flag, as shown in Table 6-2.

*Table 6-2. Style Flags Available for Integer.parse*

| Style Flag | Description |
| --- | --- |
| Flags.None | No modifiers are applied (the default) |
| Flags.Prefix | Prefix the conversion with a radix specifier |
| Flags.Plus | Prefix positive numbers with a plus sign (+) |
| Flags.Space | Prefix positive numbers with a space |
| Flags.Zero | Pad with zeros on the left |

The following example shows how you can format a number into hexadecimals including a prefix:

```
auto text = Integer.format (new char[32], 12345L, Style.HexUpper, Flags.Prefix);
```

---

Note ➡ In the example of formatting numbers as hexadecimals, `tango.text.convert.Integer` has been imported using renamed imports, so that the operations in the module can be used through the `Integer` namespace.

---

Along with `parse` and `format`, the `Integer` module contains some convenience functions. `toString`, `toString16`, and `toString32` will format a number for you, allocating the necessary storage as it goes along. `toInt` and `toLong` will parse a string, assuming that it is fully parsable.

You can also use `convert`, which does not look for a radix in the input text. The `trim` function will extract optional signs and the radix, while removing extraneous space at the start, leaving the digits ready for parsing.

## Converting Floating-Point Numbers

For the various floating-point types in D—`float`, `double`, and `real`—you should use `tango.text.convert.Float` to convert between them and their text representations. This module is somewhat simpler to use than `Integer`, as there are fewer variations in how the results can be formatted.

`parse` normally takes only the string representing the number, but can take an additional pointer to a `uint`, which will represent how much of the string was processed (or eaten) to create the resulting numeric type.

When formatting a floating-point number using `format`, you can customize it using two additional parameters. The first parameter after the number to be formatted is the number of decimals to be used. The default is 6. The second parameter is an `int` indicating how many exponent places should be emitted, effectively saying at which point a number should start being formatted in scientific notation. You can use 0 for always and 2 for numbers larger than 100 or smaller than 0.01. The default is 10. Here is an example of formatting a floating-point number:

```
auto text = Float.format (new char[64], 223.1456667, 5, 2);
```

This will convert the number into a string using five decimal places and scientific notation: `2.23145e+02`. The result will be a slice from the buffer, which is created on the heap in this example. Also in this example, the renaming of imports is used to create the `Float` namespace.

As with `Integer`, `Float` has wrappers for the most common setup, negating the need to preallocate a buffer for the output. `toString`, `toString16`, and `toString32` wrap `format`, whereas `toDouble` wraps the parsing, requiring that the full string is parsable as a number.

## Converting Dates

Strings representing points in time can also be converted into a numeric value, a so-called *timestamp*, by importing `tango.text.convert.TimeStamp`. The resulting value is usually how many units of time have passed since a particular point, called an *epoch*. The most common type of timestamp in modern computing has been the number of milliseconds since 1970.

You can pass a string to `parse` in one of the formats specified in Table 6-3, getting a timestamp in return. The one additional optional parameter is a pointer to a `uint` saying how much of the string was parsed to create the timestamp. If the parsing fails, the predefined value `InvalidEpoch` will be returned instead.

*Table 6-3. Some Ttimestamp Formats Handled by tango.text.convert.TimeStamp*

| Format | Example |
| --- | --- |
| RFC 1123 | Sun, 06 Nov 1994 08:49:37 GMT |
| RFC 850 | Sunday, 06-Nov-94 08:49:37 GMT |
| asctime | Sun Nov 6 08:49:37 1994 |
| DOS time | 12-31-06 08:49AM |
| ISO-8601 | 2006-01-31 14:49:30,001 |

Formatting a timestamp using `format` will yield a string in the RFC 1123 format. `toString`, `toString16`, and `toString32` wrap this for the cases where you don't want to or don't need to preallocate a buffer for the output. The following example shows a string that is parsed before the resulting value is formatted.

```
auto date = "Sun, 06 Nov 1994 08:49:37 GMT";
auto msSinceJan1st0001 = TimeStamp.parse (date);
auto text = TimeStamp.format (new char[64], msSinceJan1st0001);
```

dostime and iso8601 can be used to convert from the DOS time and ISO-8601 formats, respectively. rfc1123, rfc850, and asctime do the work for parse, and can be used directly if you are sure of the format of the timestamp's textual representation.

---

Tip ➡ See tango.time.ISO8601 for a more complete module for ISO-8601 parsing.

---

# Layout and Formatting

As part of the Tango text-processing functionality, you will find a powerful text-formatting framework. It replaces what has typically been done by printf in C and related languages, and is similar to the formatting frameworks of .NET and ICU. Tango's formatter is more flexible in how it can format. Tango itself uses the flexibility of the formatting system to extend it for locale support.

The formatter is accessible through several levels in Tango, depending on your needs. You will find the core functionality in tango.text.convert.Layout, whereas tango.io.Stdout provides formatting to the console, similar to printf. Stdout again utilizes tango.io.Print, which wraps Layout for all cases where you need to send formatted output to a stream. In addition, you can also use tango.text.convert.Sprint, which wraps Layout for heapless formatting, reusing memory from the construction of the Sprint instance, whether this is allocated on the heap or the stack. Layout is also supported in the tango.util.log package and via tango.io.stream.FormatStream for generic stream output.

In this section, first we will cover the format string and how it can be composed, then the Layout class, and finally, the Locale extension.

## The Format String

If you are going to print a formatted string to the console, you will typically do so using Stdout, as in the following example:

```
import tango.io.Stdout;
Stdout.format ("Printing the value {} to the {}", 5, "console").newline;
```

Here, the first string passed to format is the format string. It describes how you want your output to look, with the braces ({}) as placeholders for dynamic content. In this example, the first pair of braces will be substituted with 5 and the second with console.

Typically, you will want to specify your output in more detail and also say something about where in the template the arguments should be put. The newline at the end emits a newline and flushes Stdout so that the message is seen on the console immediately.

A number within the braces functions as a zero-based index into format's argument list. Thus, the previous format call is equivalent to this:

```
Stdout.format ("Printing the value {0} to the {1}", 5, "console").newline;
```

Since the order for the example already is implicit, there is not much point to using this technique here. The line can be rewritten to the following:

```
Stdout.format ("Printing the value {1} to the {0}", "console", 5).newline;
```

The output will be the same, but now the second argument after the format string is used first. This becomes particularly useful when internationalizing your application. By passing format strings from different languages, and having a fixed order of the arguments, you can use the indices to make the words of the different languages be printed in a sane and correct order. The following example shows how this is done with an English phrase, where the second form tends to be more common in poetry, "I can see Bill" versus "Bill I can see."

```
char[] s = "I";   // subject
char[] o = "Bill"; // object
Stdout.format ("{0} can see {1}.", s, o).newline;
Stdout.format ("{1} {0} can see.", s, o).newline;
```

An index can also be reused several times so that a particular value can be repeated, as follows:

```
Stdout.format ("Printing the value {0} and then the same again {0}", 5);
```

---

Note ➡ If you need to print a brace, escape it with another one, like this {{.

---

A pair of braces is called a *format item*, and can contain up to three components, all of which are optional. The first one is the index (as shown in the previous example), the second is an alignment component, and the third is a format string component. Let's take a closer look at the latter two components.

## Alignment Component

You can use the alignment component of a format item to specify how much space a format item should take in the resulting string. The default is that the formatter uses as much space as is needed. If the alignment component specifies less than is actually needed, the specified value will be ignored. If more than needed is specified, the remaining space will be padded.

Alignment is specified by a number directly preceded by a comma, thus an index plus alignment component will become {index,alignment}. Here's an example:

```
char[] myFName = "Johnny";
Stdout.formatln("First Name = |{0,15}|", myFName);
Stdout.formatln("Last Name = |{0,15}|", "Foo de Bar");

Stdout.formatln("First Name = |{0,-15}|", myFName);
Stdout.formatln("Last Name = |{0,-15}|", "Foo de Bar");

Stdout.formatln("First name = |{0,5}|", myFName);
```

An additional aspect of the alignment component is shown in the third and fourth calls to formatln. (Stdout.formatln emits an additional newline at the end of the output, but is otherwise the same as format; this is an alternative to adding newline at the end.) By negating the alignment, the printed text will be left-adjusted instead of being put to the right (the default). In other words, negation will pad behind, while the default behavior is to pad in front of the value. The output of the preceding example will look like this:

```
First Name = |         Johnny|
Last Name = |     Foo de Bar|
First Name = |Johnny         |
Last Name = |Foo de Bar     |
First name = |Johnny|
```

On the last line of this output, you can see how the alignment is ignored, as the amount of space specified wasn't enough to output the value Johnny.

## Format String Component

To apply additional cues to the formatter, you can use a format string component within the braces of the format item. When specifying it, prepend it with a colon, as in the following example:

```
Stdout.formatln ("I have {:G} birds on the roof", 100);
```

In the example, the letter G is used, which stands for General and is also the default used if nothing is specified.

The format string component does not need to be only one letter. It can also be a string to indicate a more complex specification. Subclasses of Layout, such as Locale, can add support for more format string components or reinterpret, such as for localization purposes.

Table 6-4 shows which format components are supported for Layout.

*Table 6-4. Supported Format String Components in tango.text.convert.Layout*

| Format | Description |
| --- | --- |
| d | Decimal format (default) |
| x | Hexadecimal format |
| X | Uppercase hexadecimal format |
| e, E | Scientific notation |

Appending a positive number immediately after one of the format components listed in Table 6-4 will give the minimum number of digits used to format the number. Here is an example:

```
Stdout.formatln ("A hexadecimal number follows: {0:X9}", 0xafe0000);
```

This will print an uppercase hexadecimal number using nine digits: 00AFE0000.

## The Layout Class

When you are formatting using Tango, tango.text.convert.Layout does most of the work in its convert method, or sprint when you want to format to a preallocated buffer. For sprint, the first argument should be the output, and the format string should be the second buffer. For convert, the format string is first. The arguments following the format string are those that will be formatted and substituted into the template string.

If you need to format a string, but don't want to print it to the console, you can instantiate Layout directly. convert is aliased to Layout's opCall, thus you can format as in this example:

```
import tango.text.convert.Layout;
auto layout = new Layout!(char); // Need to specify encoding you are going to use
auto result = layout("A format {}", "string");
```

If you want to format text in a different encoding, you can use the `fromUtf8`, `fromUtf16`, or `fromUtf32` method.

---

Tip ➡ `tango.text.convert.Format` contains a Layout already instantiated for UTF-8.

---

# Locale Support

The locale support works by subclassing `Layout`, hooking into the various format string components, and specifying a lot more functionality. To use `Locale`, you just need to instantiate it instead of `Layout`.

```
import tango.text.locale.Locale;
auto locale = new Locale;
```

Note that `Locale` has UTF-8 set as its default encoding. To enable localized output using `Stdout`, set it as the layout engine using `Stdout`'s layout property, as follows:

```
Stdout.layout = new Locale;
```

If nothing more is specified, `Locale` will try to look up the locale settings of the user's computer and format according to what it finds. If you want to specify a specific locale setting, do this via `Locale`'s constructor, as follows:

```
auto locale = new Locale(Culture.getCulture("fr_FR"));
```

The format string components that are understood by `Locale` when given a numeric value are shown in Table 6-5.

*Table 6-5. Format String Components for tango.text.locale.Locale for Numeric Values*

| Format | Description |
| --- | --- |
| g, G | General (default) |
| d, D | Decimal |
| x, X | Lowercase and uppercase hexadecimal |

*(Continued)*

| Format | Description |
|--------|-------------|
| b, B | Binary string |
| c, C | Currency |
| f, F | Fixed-point |
| n, N | Number with a delimiter (, or .) every three digits |

All the format string components support an additional number to specify the precision of the formatted number.

The other kind of values localized by `Locale` are `tango.time.Time.Time` objects. Table 6-6 shows which format string components are available as shortcuts when a `Time` instance is passed to the formatter. These shortcuts are substituted with a pattern in the formatter.

*Table 6-6. Format String Components for tango.text.locale.Locale for Time Values*

| Format[a] | Description | Pattern |
|-----------|-------------|---------|
| d | Short date | dd/MM/yyyy |
| D | Long date | dddd dd MMMM yyyy. |
| f | Long date and short time | dddd dd MMMM yyyy HH': 'mm |
| F | Full date and time | dddd dd MMMM yyyy HH': 'mm': 'ss |
| g | Short date and short time | dd/MM/yyyy HH': 'mm |
| G | Short date and long time | dd/MM/yyyy HH': 'mm': 'ss |
| m, M | Day in month | MM MMMM |
| r, R | RFC 1123 | ddd, dd MMM yyyy HH': 'mm': 'ss 'GMT'" |
| s | A sortable date time | yyyy'-'MM'-'dd'T'HH': 'mm': 'ss" |

*(Continued)*

| Format[a] | Description | Pattern |
|---|---|---|
| t | Short time | HH': 'mm |
| T | Long time | HH': 'mm': 'ss |
| y, Y | Month in year | MMMM yyyy |

[a]*This format is locale-independent. If a locale for a specific culture is chosen, the format may vary.*

If the format string component for a `Time` instance is more than one character, it means that it is a custom format, which may include the components shown in Table 6-7. The patterns shown in Table 6-6 are predefined examples of such patterns. Elements in these patterns that are enclosed in single quotation marks are printed as is. This is mainly used to escape parts of the pattern that otherwise may be interpreted in some capacity by the formatter.

*Table 6-7. Custom Formatting Options for Time Instances*

| Format | Description |
|---|---|
| dddd | Full name of the day in the week |
| ddd | The name of day in the week, three letters |
| dd | The day in the month, two digits |
| MMMM | Full name of month |
| MMM | Short name of month, four letters |
| MM | Month in the year, two digits |
| yy, yyyy | Year, two or four digits |
| HH | Hours |
| mm | Minutes |
| ss | Seconds |

The following is an example of printing a `Time` instance to the console in a customized format, using direct console output via `tango.io.Console.Cout`.

```
import tango.io.Console;
import tango.time.WallClock;
import tango.text.locale.Locale;

auto layout = new Locale;
Cout (layout ("{:ddd, dd MMMM yyyy HH':'mm':'ss z}", WallClock.now)).newline;
```

You should by now have a good understanding of the basic and intermediate routines present in Tango's text-processing functionality. In the next chapter, you'll learn about Tango's input/output packages.

# CHAPTER 7

# Input and Output

Tango offers a broad range of functionality for handling input/output (I/O). In this chapter, we introduce four principal features of the `tango.io` package:

- Console I/O

- Stream I/O

- Network I/O

- File handling.

First, let's get a couple of definitions out of the way. If you already familiar with the notion of *streams*, feel free to skip ahead.

Tango I/O is primarily stream-oriented. A stream represents a contiguous flow of data without any particular format or discernible feature. Applications may subsequently apply type or semantic structure (meaning) to the data, perhaps treating it as a set of records or lines of text. However, the flow is just a meaningless set of bytes at the raw stream level. Perhaps one common characteristic of a stream is that it usually terminates at some point.

One end of each stream in a Tango program typically connects to some external device, such as a file, network connection, or console. Within the Tango library, these stream end points are known as *conduits*, and each plays host to both an input and output stream for the specific device. If you conceptualize that each device has a pair of streams attached, you have the notion of a conduit all squared away.

## Console I/O

The console is where text output from your program will often be displayed. Console support in Tango is stream-oriented, and includes a high-level type-conversion layer along with a lightweight UTF-8 interface. The former includes `Stdout` and `Stderr`; the latter consists of `Cout`, `Cerr`, and `Cin`. We discuss each of them here, starting with the lightweight interface.

# Console Output Using Cout and Cerr

Perhaps the simplest way to display text on the console is via either `Cout` or `Cerr`. These are predefined entities in `tango.io.Console` that route `char[]` content to the appropriate output device. Here's an example:

```
import tango.io.Console;
Cout ("the quick brown fox").newline;
```

The `newline` appended in this example causes the output to be flushed. Line breaks may be embedded within the literal also, using the traditional \n syntax, though these are simply passed along by Tango; no explicit processing is performed. Console output is buffered, so without a `newline`, the text would not be sent to the destination immediately. Where line breaks are inappropriate, you can achieve immediate flushing to the console by using `Cout("hello").flush` or the shortcut variant `Cout("hello")()`, where the empty parentheses indicate a flush operation.

Console methods return a chaining reference, enabling the following style for those who prefer it:

```
auto action = "jumps over the lazy dog";
Cout ("the quick brown fox ")(action).newline;
```

---

Note ➡ The console does not directly support formatted output. Each argument is processed independently and rendered to the output in a simple left-to-right order. You can use a `Layout` or `Print` instance to generate formatted `Cout` output, which is just what `Stdout` does on your behalf.

---

Object references may be passed to `Cout`, where the object will be queried to obtain a literal:

```
auto o = new Object;
Cout ("the name of Object is ")(o).newline;
```

Console elements expose their underlying stream in order to permit more expressive usage. For example, the following is a shortcut for copying a text file to the console:

```
import tango.io.Console;
import tango.io.stream.FileStream;

Cout.stream.copy (new FileInput ("myfile"));
```

## Console Input with Cin

Console input is enabled in a manner similar to Cout, but using the predefined entity Cin instead. Tango waits for some input to be available and returns all of it to the caller. With interactive console usage, this is usually one line of input, returned by the operating system whenever the Enter key is pressed. Here is an example:

```
import tango.io.Console;

Cout ("What is your name? ").flush;
auto name = Cin.readln;
Cout ("Hello ")(name).newline;
```

Where console redirection has been applied (via a pipe or equivalent mechanism), Cin will relay large quantities of redirected input back to the caller for each invocation. You can split the resultant input stream into lines of text, for example, by applying a LineStream to the stream exposed by Cin:

```
import tango.io.Console;
import tango.io.stream.LineStream;

foreach (line; new LineInput(Cin.stream))
        Cout (line).newline;
```

As you can see, this shows the console being used purely as a streaming input source. Cin already has embedded support for reading discrete lines of text via its readln and copyln methods, but a LineInput can often be convenient. Consider using a stream iterator from the tango.text.stream package when you need to split text on boundaries other than lines.

In order to ensure platform independence, and to accommodate console redirection across a variety of use cases, all console-based interaction should be UTF-8 only. The console device interface handles potential conversion between UTF-8 and a platform-specific encoding. Instances of IOException are thrown when the underlying operating system determines an error occurred, such as when redirection ran into a problem with a remote file.

---

Tip ➡ You can transfer console input to output by copying `Cin` to `Cout` as follows: `Cout.stream.copy (Cin.stream)`.

---

## Formatted Output Using Stdout and Stderr

`Stdout` is a general-purpose formatter, sitting atop `Cout`. There's also a `Stderr` tied to `Cerr`, and both are predefined within the `tango.io.Stdout` module. Where `Cout` supports UTF-8 only, `Stdout` handles a wide range of types, converting from native representation to text for display purposes and translating text represented by UTF-16 and/or UTF-32 into the format expected by the console.

The core formatting functionality is provided by `tango.text.convert.Layout` and exposed through `Stdout` via a number of convenience methods. These methods return a chaining reference (like much of the library does) and accept multiple arguments in the conventional variable argument (vararg) style. For example, a formatted vararg call looks like this:

```
import tango.io.Stdout;

Stdout.format ("{} green bottles, sitting on the wall", 10).newline;
```

Flushing the output without a line break is similar to `Cout`, using either `flush` or an empty set of parentheses like so:

```
Stdout.format ("{} green bottles, sitting on the wall", 10) ();
```

There is also a variant to append a `newline`, which itself implies a flush:

```
Stdout.formatln ("{} green bottles, sitting on the wall", 10);
```

---

Note ➡ A `newline` implies a flush when console I/O is not redirected, causing immediate rendering of `Stdout` text to a typical console. I/O redirection inhibits this automatic flush behavior, in order to increase throughput. `Cout` operates in a similar manner.

---

Table 7-1 lists some of the variations available for `Stdout`, with the results shown on the right.

*Table 7-1. Some Stdout Variations*

| Usage Style | Result |
| --- | --- |
| Stdout ("Hello"); | Hello |
| Stdout (1); | 1 |
| Stdout (3.14159); | 3.14 |
| Stdout ('B'); | B |
| Stdout (1, 2, 3); | 1, 2, 3 |
| Stdout ("abc", 1, 2, 3); | abc, 1, 2, 3 |
| Stdout ("abc", 1, 2) ("foo"); | abc, 1, 2foo |
| Stdout ("abc") ("def") (3.14); | abcdef3.14 |
| Stdout.format ("abc {} '{}'", 1, 2); | abc 1 '2' |

Stdout.format supports a variety of options. Unlike C's printf, Stdout already knows the type of each argument provided, rendering the printf type specifier obsolete. Instead, Stdout supports an optional format descriptor. A portion of the descriptor is generic across all types, while the rest is specific to a particular argument type. It has the following structure:

'{' [index] [',' alignment] [':' format] '}'

The curly braces are required. alignment indicates a minimum layout width that should be negative to indicate left alignment. The colon is a required prefix for any type-specific option. An optional index indicates which argument is being addressed. The latter can become important when considering internationalization and localization, where the format strings (including embedded indices) might be externalized and adjusted for locale specifics. Table 7-2 shows some examples of formatted output.

*Table 7-2. Formatting Examples*

| Format Syntax | Result |
|---|---|
| Stdout.format ("{} {}", "hello", "world"); | hello world |
| Stdout.format ("{1} {0}", "hello", "world"); | world hello |
| Stdout.format ("\|{,10}\|", "hello"); | \|     hello\| |
| Stdout.format ("\|{,-10}\|", "hello"); | \|hello     \| |
| Stdout.format ("0x{:x}", 32); | 0x20 |
| Stdout.format ("0x{:x4}", 32); | 0x0020 |
| Stdout.format ("0b{:b4}", 5); | 0b0101 |
| Stdout.format ("{:f2}", 3.14159); | 3.14 |
| Stdout.format ("abc ", x); | abc |

Although Stdout.format("abc ", x) does not reference the provided argument x, it does not produce an error, since there are cases where dropping an argument is legitimate.

Like Cout and Cerr, Stdout and Stderr expose the underlying output stream, which may be used directly where appropriate. Revisiting a Cout example:

```
import tango.io.Stdout;
import tango.io.stream.FileStream;

auto file = new FileInput ("myfile");
Stdout.stream.copy (file);
```

Or, you could sidestep all formatting conversion and append content directly to the underlying stream:

```
Stdout.stream.write ("the quick brown fox jumps over the lazy dog");
```

Stdout also exposes the Layout instance in use, so that you can invoke it directly. For example, it can sometimes be useful to construct an interim array of formatted output:

```
char[128] output;
auto string = Stdout.layout.sprint (output, "{} green bottles", 10);
```

It is also possible to substitute the attached Layout instance, which is useful for configuring Stdout and Stderr with an alternate formatting handler. For example, Tango provides a locale-configurable layout, which can be substituted for the default one:

```
import tango.io.Stdout;
import tango.text.locale.Locale;

Stdout.layout = new Locale (Culture.getCulture ("fr-FR"));
```

As a layout replacement, Locale supports additional, regional-specific formatting options for currency, decimal and numeric representation, and date/time formatting. Both Layout and Locale are discussed in Chapter 6.

---

Tip ➡ Stdout functionality is supported via a module named tango.io.Print, which may be used to bind similar functionality to streams other than those tied to Cout and Cerr (such as a file or a network connection).

---

Issues arising during formatting are generally injected into the output stream in place of a formatted argument and delimited by a pair of braces. To demonstrate, try printing a null reference:

```
import tango.io.Stdout;

Object o = null;
Stdout.formatln ("using a {} object", o);
```

The following should appear on the console:

---

```
using a {null} object
```

---

# Stream I/O

Streams are utilized throughout tango.io, so a little knowledge of how they operate will put you in good stead. The two stream types represent input from a device and output to a device, named InputStream and OutputStream, respectively. Both have a simple interface, where an output stream is represented by five methods and an input stream by just four.

Both stream types have a close method, which closes the stream, and both have a conduit method to return a representation of the attached device.

An input stream has two more methods called read and clear. The former reads content into a supplied array and returns the number of bytes consumed from the input device. The latter ensures that any buffered input data is cleared away.

An output stream has three additional methods: write, flush, and copy. You've already seen copy applied a few times (from prior examples in the "Console I/O" section) where an input stream was being copied to the console output stream. Connecting streams together in this way is quite common, and copy is there to handle the chore efficiently. The other two methods are for writing an array of content to an attached device and for flushing buffered output.

Like the read method, write returns the number of bytes consumed by the output device. In both cases, the quantity consumed may be less than offered; that is, read may not fill the provided array entirely, and write may not consume all of its provided data in one gulp. In particular, both methods will return the reserved value Eof when a stream concludes.

One of the more useful aspects of streams is that they can be connected together to form processing chains, or conversion chains, utilizing a design called the *decorator pattern*. In many cases, as you'll see shortly, a predefined chain will be available for use. You can easily construct your own chains (and your own stream derivatives) if the need arises.

## Streaming Files

With all that out of the way, let's dig into the tango.io.stream facilities. For the most part, they represent predecorated streams, or wrappers around other I/O functionality. We'll start with file access, since that's a common need, and quickly step through the other modules. Here, we copy a file to the console output:

```
import tango.io.Console,
       tango.io.stream.FileStream;

auto input = new FileInput ("myfile");
Cout.stream.copy (input);
input.close;
```

This snippet copies console input to a file:

```
import tango.io.Console,
       tango.io.stream.FileStream;

auto output = new FileOutput ("myfile");
```

```
output.copy (Cin.stream);
output.close;
```

Note that you should always close the stream when finished with it. In this next example, we use TextFileStream to read lines of text, one at a time, and write each to the console:

```
import tango.io.Console,
       tango.io.stream.TextFileStream;

auto input = new TextFileInput ("myfile");
foreach (line; input)
         Cout(line).flush;
input.close;
```

Here, we write formatted text to an output file, again using TextFileStream. The formatting functionality mirrors that of Stdout:

```
import tango.io.Console,
       tango.io.stream.TextFileStream;

auto output = new TextFileOutput ("myfile");
output.formatln ("{} green bottles", 10);
output.flush.close;
```

Flushing an output stream before closing it is generally a good idea, unless the stream is being discarded. In this next variation, an input stream is copied explicitly, so you can see how to use the read function:

```
import tango.io.Console,
       tango.io.stream.FileStream;

char[1024] tmp;
int        len;

auto input = new FileInput("myfile");
while ((len = input.read(tmp)) != input.Eof)
        Cout (tmp[0 .. len]).flush;
input.close;
```

It is certainly less work to use copy instead! An alternative would be to decorate the stream with a filter that consumes everything it is asked to read or write:

```
import tango.io.Console,
       tango.io.stream.FileStream,
       tango.io.stream.GreedyStream;
```

```
auto output = new GreedyOutput (new FileOutput("myfile"));
output.write ("the quick brown fox jumps over the lazy dog");
output.flush.close;
```

We wrapped the file stream inside a greedy stream (so they are now chained together), and each request to the greedy stream is relayed to its contained file stream. It's called *greedy* because it consumes everything asked of it, instead of consuming only what it can. We still flush the output before closing, though in this case, it is not strictly necessary.

This next example demonstrates binary I/O using `DataFileStream`, which also supports random access (file seeking). Because of the random-access aspect, this code requires a bit of knowledge not discussed until later in this chapter, in the "Accessing File Content Using FileConduit" section, but we'll go ahead and show how it operates anyway:

```
import tango.io.FileConduit,
       tango.io.stream.DataFileStream;

auto file = new FileConduit ("myfile", FileConduit.ReadWriteCreate);
auto input = new DataFileInput (file);
auto output = new DataFileOutput (file);

int x=10, y=20;
output.putInt(x);
output.putInt(y);
output.seek (0);

x = input.getInt;
y = input.getInt;
file.close;
```

The interesting elements here include the `FileConduit` (a device) representing a seekable read-write file, and the data-oriented streams that operate on it.

---

Note ➡ `DateFileStream` also buffers the I/O (you may set the buffer size via the streams), and the seek method flushes the output before adjusting the file location.

---

Lastly, the following is an example of a stream decorator to read and write maps (hash tables) of name/value pairs. We use it to write to a text file and then read the pairs back again into another map. The content of the file will be a series of name=value tuples, separated by a line ending.

```
import tango.io.stream.MapStream,
```

```
        tango.io.stream.FileStream;

char[][char[]] settings;
settings ["server-port"] = "8080";
settings ["log-file"] = "log/all.log";
settings ["multicast-address"] = "225.0.0.9";

auto output = new MapOutput (new FileOutput("myfile"));
output.append(settings).flush.close;

char[][char[]] copy;
auto input = new MapInput (new FileInput("myfile"));
input.load (copy);
input.close;
```

# A Fistful of Streams

There are more streaming facilities where those just discussed came from, and they can be applied directly to any old stream, rather than just a file. For example, you can also attach MapStream onto the console, a network connection, or a memory-based stream. The same goes for LineStream, FormatStream, GreedyStream, TypedStream, UtfStream, SnoopStream, DigestStream, DataStream, and EndianStream. These are all decorators intended for chaining onto another stream, and we'll briefly describe a handful of them here.

FormatStream provides an output formatter just like Stdout, but for binding to any other stream. The TextFileOutput discussed earlier derives from FormatStream, which itself is derived from tango.io.Print.

TypedStream treats streams as a set of (templated) types. In other words, it enables you to address a stream as a set of discrete characters, integers, structs, or whatever the stream comprises.

UtfStream converts from one UTF encoding to another. For instance, you can use it to convert a UTF-8 stream into a UTF-32 stream and vice versa. Use it in conjunction with an EndianStream in order to add endian (byte-order) conversion where applicable.

DigestStream attaches a digest to a provided stream, and updates the digest as data flows by. The tango.io.digest package contains a selection of message-digest algorithms, including MD2, MD4, MD5, SHA0, SHA1, SHA01, SHA256, SHA512, and Tiger. These can be hooked to DigestStream as a convenient means of stream processing.

SnoopStream generates debug messages describing the operations being performed on it. By doing so, SnoopStream can provide introspection into stream behavior; it snoops on the data flow.

# Streams of Memory

BufferStream provides the equivalent of a cache for streaming content, enabling an underlying device to be read and written in large chunks instead of discrete data elements. This can optimize many common operations, such as token parsing or output concatenation, and can support efficient mapping of data-record content into program memory.

BufferStream itself is a shallow wrapper around a generic buffering module called Buffer, which can be used directly also. In addition to supporting the pedestrian stream operations, Buffer exposes a range of functionality from simple append operations to more prosaic producer/consumer balancing between streams of different bandwidths. Buffer also supports multiple downstream consumers. For instance, several contiguous stream iterators may be attached at one time (see the next section), and Buffer will maintain common state across them. However, typical usage is just regular buffering of either file or network I/O:

```
import tango.io.stream.FileStream,
       tango.io.stream.BufferStream;

auto input = new BufferInput (new FileInput("myfile"));
```

Buffer is data type-agnostic and operates as a smart array, flushing and/or refilling itself via connected upstreams as necessary. Buffer is actually a conduit instance for a pseudodevice, and exposes both an input stream and an output stream. You can thus connect various stream decorators in order to imply structure over the content therein.

When using TextFileStream, DataFileStream, or various other decorators, buffering will be initiated on your behalf. In other cases, you may find that manually applying BufferStream is a more convenient option (perhaps for your own decorators). The wrappers discussed exist so you generally don't need to glue the various pieces together yourself, yet Buffer is the mechanism they apply under the covers.

While a Buffer is often attached to an upstream device (such as a network connection or file), it can happily be used in stand-alone fashion as a memory-based accumulator. There is one distinction between the two usage scenarios: without an upstream device (such as a file), the buffer cannot be automatically flushed when filled to capacity, so an exception will be raised when this occurs. You can use an expanding buffer called GrowBuffer to handle cases where no upstream device is connected and output content is expected to grow in size. Here's an example of both buffer variations used in a stand-alone mode:

```
import tango.io.Buffer,
       tango.io.Console;

auto buffer = new Buffer ("Hello World\n");
Cout.stream.copy (buffer);
```

```
buffer = new GrowBuffer;
buffer.append("Hello ").append(" World\n");
Cout.stream.copy (buffer);
```

Another `Buffer` variant, `MappedBuffer`, wraps operating system facilities to expose memory-mapped files. The buffer memory is mapped directly onto a (usually) large file, which you can then treat as just another stream. You can even treat `MappedBuffer` content directly as a native array.

## Stream Iterators

Tango has a set of classes to split streaming text input into elements bounded by a specific pattern. These classes reside in `tango.text.stream` and are templated for `char`, `wchar`, and `dchar` data types. They include an iterator for producing lines of text based on finding embedded end-of-line markers, as well as iterators for isolating text patterns, delimiters, quoted strings, and so on.

For example, you might convert an input stream of characters into a series of lines. We use a `Buffer` instance here, but you can use any input stream:

```
import tango.io.Console;
import tango.text.stream.LineIterator;

auto input = new Buffer("Hello\n World\n");
foreach (line; new LineIterator!(char)(input))
        Cout(line).newline;
```

If this looks familiar, then it's likely because the `LineStream` example shown previously is a simple wrapper around the templated class.

Each stream iterator will generate an `IOException` when the size of a single element is larger than the containing `Buffer`. This might be because that buffer is too small or an element is overly large. You could increase the buffer size to accommodate very large elements (a typical I/O buffer is 8KB or 16KB).

---

Tip ➡ Iterator results are usually aliased directly from an underlying buffer, thus avoiding considerable heap activity where an application doesn't need it. When the resultant element is to be retained by the application, it should be copied before iteration continues (using `.dup` or equivalent).

---

# Network I/O

In this section, you'll get a general overview of network support and how it fits into the overall I/O framework. The support provided by Tango is intended to expose aspects of network programming in a simple and straightforward manner, while providing the means to reach underlying mechanisms where necessary.

---

Tip ➡ A number of excellent generic network-programming tutorials are available on the Internet. To learn more, try http://beej.us/guide/bgnet.

---

## Creating an InternetAddress

An address/port pair describes an Internet location, and this is encapsulated within an InternetAddress. The address may refer to the hosting computer (a local address) or to some machine on the other side of the globe.

Local addresses are often used by applications acting as a destination for other machines (as a listener, or server), whereas remote addresses are generally used to enable a program (client) to make resource requests of a server machine. While the address and port of a remote location must be described explicitly, both may be implied for a local location by leaving them unspecified. Sometimes it is convenient to use the hosting machine as both a listening server and a client. In such cases, the remote address would effectively map to the local address (directly or indirectly).

InternetAddress is a required parameter for a number of other network-oriented classes, and it is simple to construct. Creating an Internet reference to the Digital Mars web server, for example, can be accomplished like so, using the domain name along with the port number reserved for HTTP servers:

```
import tango.net.InternetAddress;
```

```
auto addr = new InternetAddress ("www.digitalmars.com", 80);
```

Alternatively, this could be constructed using a numeric address:

```
auto addr = new InternetAddress ("65.204.18.192", 80);
```

A third, and often convenient, alternative is to append the port number to the address descriptor itself:

```
auto addr = new InternetAddress ("www.digitalmars.com:80");
```

Each of these alternatives maps to the same remote location. On the server end, to create a local address for listening purposes, you could use this variation with no arguments:

```
auto addr = new InternetAddress;
```

With no explicit arguments, both the address and port will be assigned and configured on your behalf. To request a specific port (such as port 80), use this signature instead:

```
auto addr = new InternetAddress (80);
```

Each of these address instances represents *potential* connectivity within your program, since there's no connection made at this time. It may turn out that a remote location is not listening or is otherwise unavailable, or it may be that a local listening address is already in use by some other server. These issues do not arise within InternetAddress itself, since it is purely an encapsulation of attributes. Instead, they may surface when using bind or connect at a later stage.

## Low-Level Socket Access

Tango wraps its underlying network functionality in a cross-platform façade named Socket, and exposes it as an attribute of higher-level constructs such as SocketConduit. As such, Socket represents a low-level network interface in Tango.

Within Socket, you'll find methods to directly manipulate the socket transport layer and associated controls. For example, switching between blocking and nonblocking sockets remains in the realm of Socket, as does domain-name lookup, select requests, socket-connectivity options, and other lower-level machinations.

In general, it is preferable to rely on higher-level constructs such as SocketConduit and ServerSocket to configure and manipulate the underlying socket on your behalf. However, the higher levels provide access to the Socket instance for use when you need to dig a little deeper.

## Using TCP/IP Streams with SocketConduit

SocketConduit represents the gateway to a TCP/IP network. It is oriented toward blocking operations (for example, it will potentially stall while waiting for input to arrive), although it can operate in a limited nonblocking configuration. It is a true instance of a Tango conduit and thus exposes both an input stream and an output stream for general usage. For instance, you could copy file content to a network location in the following manner:

```
import tango.net.SocketConduit,
       tango.net.InternetAddress;
import tango.io.stream.FileStream;

auto host = new SocketConduit;
host.connect (new InternetAddress ("www.myhost.com", myport));
host.output.copy (new FileInput ("myfile"));
```

When reading from a network, you can use a similar approach to copy content to a file, to the console, to another instance of SocketConduit, or to any other stream derivative. You could display the raw response of a web server on the console like so (using path /index.html):

```
import tango.io.Console;
import tango.net.SocketConduit,
       tango.net.InternetAddress;

auto host = new SocketConduit;
auto addr = new InternetAddress ("www.myhost.com:80");
host.connect(addr).output.write ("GET /index.html HTTP/1.0\r\n\r\n");
Cout.stream.copy (host.input);
```

---

Note ➡ Unlike FileConduit and the console, SocketConduit may require an explicit connect step in order to instantiate input and output streams. This is shown in both client examples here, whereas a server program is typically handed a SocketConduit with the streams already primed and active.

---

SocketConduit has methods to connect to an address, bind to a local adapter for listening purposes, shut down one or both associated streams, test for timeout conditions, and expose the underlying Socket instance via a socket property.

Each read operation is made under a timeout period, thus avoiding endless waiting for a remote listener to respond. The default timeout period is set at 3 seconds, which can be adjusted via a timeout method.

Because it is a stream host, SocketConduit can be used in conjunction with many of the other I/O elements such as filters, streaming iterators, buffers, and so on.

# Packet Operations with DatagramConduit

A *datagram* is a message sent over a network as a discrete User Datagram Protocol (UDP) packet, with a maximum size dictated by the network and/or the operating system. Unlike TCP/IP, UDP is an *unreliable* protocol, meaning that messages might be lost. Where TCP/IP will manage retransmission on your behalf, UDP is completely devoid of such overhead. Where TCP/IP is stream-oriented, UDP is oriented around discrete packets.

UDP can be a blessing for some data streams, where a certain amount of dropped information does not significantly impact the end result. For instance, sending real-time video over a UDP connection can save a lot of grief (in terms of maintaining the real-time aspect), as dropping a video packet here and there will often not adversely affect the desired result. On the other hand, relying on UDP to support networked financial transactions is likely to result in serious discontent for someone. Thus, UDP is useful as a low-overhead means of network communication—communication that does not require guaranteed delivery.

DatagramConduit is a derivative of SocketConduit, so you may treat it in much the same manner for most operations. The principal difference is in the distinction between data streams and discrete data packets when reading and writing. The second distinction is that both read and write accept an optional address. The write method can direct each sent packet to a different address, and the read method may receive from different addresses; that is, read returns the packet originator via an optional address provided to it. Here's an example that sends itself a datagram, using bind to initiate listening:

```
import tango.io.Console;
import tango.net.InternetAddress,
       tango.net.DatagramConduit;

// Listen for datagrams on the local address
auto gram = new DatagramConduit;
auto addr = new InternetAddress ("127.0.0.1", 8080);
gram.bind (addr);

// Write to the address. Retrieve and display message also, since we are listening
gram.write ("hello", addr);
char[8] tmp;
auto size = gram.read (tmp);
Cout (tmp[0..size]).newline;
```

Bell, et al.

# Simple Publish/Subscribe Using MulticastSocket

Network hardware is often configured with a facility to distribute datagrams across clients that have registered interest in a particular set. These *subscribers* register their interest by joining a *multicast group*, which is one of a reserved set of network addresses. Subscription is different from its *broadcast* predecessor in that the former does not receive any datagrams until a subscription has taken place. Subscription can also be relinquished and reinstated as appropriate.

---

Note ➡ Multicast subscription (and dispatch) operates on a reserved set of network addresses, called class D addresses, which range from 225.0.0.0 to 239.255.255.255 inclusive.

---

A notable benefit of both broadcast and multicast is that datagram dispersal can take place at the hardware level, making it a particularly efficient means of pushing information from a central point to many recipients. However, their application has some fairly narrow limitations, due to the network-traffic pressure that broad usage may cause. Thus, multicast distribution is usually scoped to occur within a specific number of network hops known as the *time-to-live* (TTL) of a transmission, which is typically within the local network subnet or site. Related choices for the ttl method include those listed in Table 7-3.

*Table 7-3. Multicast TTL Options*

| Name | Domain |
| --- | --- |
| Host | Restricted to the same host |
| Subnet | Restricted to the same subnet |
| Site | Restricted to the same site |
| Region | Restricted to the same region |
| Continent | Restricted to the same continent |

Other than ttl, you use MulticastConduit in a manner similar to DatagramConduit. It must be bound to an address before incoming datagrams will be noted, though this can be handled on your behalf by a class constructor. MulticastConduit adds join and leave methods, which subscribe and cancel, respectively. You can use multicast yourself in the following manner:

```
import tango.io.Console;
import tango.net.InternetAddress,
       tango.net.MulticastConduit;

auto group = new InternetAddress ("225.0.0.10:8080");

// Listen for datagrams on our group address
auto multi = new MulticastConduit (group);

// Subscribe and multicast on the group
multi.join.write ("hello", group);

// We are subscribed, and can thus see the multicast ourselves
char[8] tmp;
auto len = multi.read (tmp);
Cout (tmp[0 .. len]).newline;
```

---

Tip ➡ The example shows receipt of dispatched messages, which you can disable via a `loopback` method.

---

## Writing a TCP/IP Server with ServerSocket

A server program typically listens for network requests from clients and responds to them in some manner. In order to simplify some of the work of setup and management, Tango wraps a common listening approach in a class called ServerSocket. For instance, you can create a simple network server using ServerSocket like so:

```
import tango.net.ServerSocket,
       tango.net.InternetAddress;

auto server = new ServerSocket (new InternetAddress (80));
auto request = server.accept;
```

Each time a request is made on the server, a network connection to the requesting client is returned from accept as a SocketConduit instance. Your server would read and write that instance in a manner understood by the client, and the connection would be terminated at some point thereafter.

Bell, et al.

Communicating with a server is straightforward, as the following example demonstrates:

```
import tango.io.Console;
import tango.core.Thread;
import tango.net.ServerSocket,
       tango.net.SocketConduit,
       tango.net.InternetAddress;

const int port = 8080;

void serve()
{
        auto server = new ServerSocket (new InternetAddress(port));

        // Wait for a request, and respond with a greeting
        server.accept.output.write ("server replies 'hello'");
}

// Create server in a separate thread, and pause slightly for it to begin
(new Thread (&serve)).start;
Thread.sleep (0.250);

// Make a request of our server
auto request = new SocketConduit;
request.connect (new InternetAddress ("localhost", port));

// Wait for and display response (there is an optional timeout)
char[32] response;
auto len = request.input.read (response);
Cout (response[0 .. len]).newline;
```

This example is both a server and client within the same program, where the server runs as a separate thread of execution.

# File Handling

File handling in Tango includes path manipulation, high-level wrappers to expose simplified file access, and Unicode support, along with inspection and control over the file system itself.

---

Note ➡ In this section, the words *directory* and *folder* are used interchangeably.

---

## Accessing File Content Using FileConduit

The gateway to file content is through a `FileConduit`, which provides both streaming and random-access support. Being a conduit instance, both input and output streams are exposed. When working with file content, you'll often be leveraging a `FileConduit` instance without knowing it, since it is wrapped by various other constructs within Tango. Regardless, you may need to reference this explicitly when, for example, random file access is required.

Opening a file for reading is performed as follows:

```
auto conduit = new FileConduit ("myFilePath");
```

Opening a file for writing requires one of the styles to be specified (indicating how the file is expected to be manipulated):

```
auto conduit = new FileConduit ("myFilePath",FileConduit.WriteCreate);
```

There are a variety of predefined styles, including appending, read-only, read-write, create-always, and so on. You can define additional styles using a combination of a dozen system-level flags.

FileConduit enables direct, type-agnostic streaming access to file content. In this example, we open a file and copy it directly to the console using `Cout.stream.copy`:

```
import tango.io.Console,
       tango.io.FileConduit;

auto from = new FileConduit ("test.txt");
Cout.stream.copy (from);
```

And here we copy one file to another, using a similar approach:

```
import tango.io.FileConduit;

auto to = new FileConduit ("copy.txt", FileConduit.WriteCreate);
to.output.copy (new FileConduit ("test.txt"));
```

To load an entire file into memory, you might consider the following approach, where we open a file, create an array to house the content, and then read that content:

```
import tango.io.FileConduit;
```

```
auto file = new FileConduit ("test.txt")
auto content = new char[file.length];
auto bytesRead = file.input.read (content);
```

Conversely, you may write directly to a `FileConduit`, like so:

```
import tango.io.FileConduit;

auto to = new FileConduit ("text.txt", FileConduit.WriteCreate);
auto bytesWritten = to.output.write (content);
```

Both these examples represent the essence of what `File` (covered in the next section) performs on your behalf.

`FileConduit` supports random-access I/O also. The next example relocates the current file position using seek, and utilizes a `DataFileInput`/`DataFileOutput` pair to perform simple typed input and output:

```
import tango.io.FileConduit,
       tango.io.stream.DataFileStream;

// Open a file for reading and writing
auto file = new FileConduit ("myfile", FileConduit.ReadWriteCreate);
auto input = new DataFileInput (file);
auto output = new DataFileOutput (file);

// Write data
int x=10, y=20;
output.putInt(x);
output.putInt(y);

// Rewind to file start
output.seek (0);

// Read data back again
x = input.getInt;
y = input.getInt;
file.close;
```

Each `FileConduit` should be explicitly closed when no longer needed. It can often be convenient to use a scope expression for this purpose:

```
auto file = new FileConduit ("myFile");
scope (exit)
       file.close;
```

An IOException will be raised where a read or write operation fails entirely, or where a copy operation fails to complete. This might happen if, for example, a remote file were to suddenly become unavailable while in use.

## Reading and Writing a Complete File

File combines FileConduit and FilePath together to provide a convenient means of accessing both attributes and content. The content of a file can be read, appended, or written in a single method call. For example, to read all file content, do this:

```
import tango.io.File;

auto file = new File ("myfile");
auto content = file.read;
```

The underlying file is closed before the call returns. File must avoid making assumptions about the file content, so the preceding example returns an array of type void. When working with File, it may be necessary to cast the return value to represent the correct data type, and for text files, this is often a char[]. In this example, we take advantage of a syntactic shortcut to avoid the need for new:

```
import tango.io.File;
auto content = cast(char[]) File("myfile").read;
```

To convert a text file into a set of lines, try the following:

```
import tango.io.File;
import Text = tango.text.Util;

auto content = cast(char[]) File("myfile").read;
auto lines = Text.splitLines (content);
```

Or you can use a foreach to iterate instead:

```
foreach (line; Text.lines (content))
        Cout (line).newline;
```

Files may be set to the content of an array, or text string:

```
import tango.io.File;
auto file = new File ("myfile");
file.write ("the quick brown fox");
```

Content may be appended in a similar fashion:

```
file.append (" jumps over the lazy dog");
```

Methods belonging to `FilePath` are exposed via the `path` attribute, so you can retrieve the file size, relocate it, remove it, and so on:

```
auto size = file.path.fileSize;
```

`File` will throw an `IOException` where an underlying operating system or file system error occurs. This might happen, for example, when an attempt is made to write to a read-only file.

## Working with UnicodeFile

Unicode is the standard that assigns every known symbol a unique number. The Unicode Transformation Formats, commonly referred to as UTF-8, UTF-16, and UTF-32, describe how Unicode text is actually encoded. All three of these formats are supported directly by the D language via the `char[]`, `wchar[]`, and `dchar[]` data types.

When working with Unicode files, you need to know which encoding was applied when the file was written so that it may be decoded correctly. Some text files might be of a "known" encoding, where the generating application is subsequently used to read the content. Conversely, the content of other text files might be generated by one application and read by another, where the latter is not explicitly aware of the encoding applied. Such a scenario would appear to require some kind of metadata associated with each file, in order for subsequent reading applications to "know" how the content was originally written.

Without general, cross-platform support for file-oriented metadata being available, other schemes have been applied to file content in order to identify the encoding in use. One such scheme uses the first few bytes of a file to identify the encoding, called a *byte-order mark* (BOM). For better or worse, this particular scheme has become reasonably prevalent and is thus supported within the Tango library as a convenient way to deal with Unicode-based files.

`UnicodeFile` combines facilities from the previously described `File` class with a capability to recognize and translate file content between various Unicode encodings and their native D representations. `UnicodeFile` can be explicitly told which encoding should be applied to a file, or it can discover an existing encoding via file inspection. For example, to read UTF-8 content from a file with unknown encoding, do this:

```
import tango.io.UnicodeFile;
```

```
auto file = new UnicodeFile!(char)("myfile.txt", Encoding.Unknown);
char[] content = file.read;
```

The UnicodeFile class is templated for types of char, wchar, and dchar, representing UTF-8, UTF-16, and UTF-32 encodings. Those are considered to be the *internal* encoding, while the file itself is described by an *external* encoding. In the preceding example, our external encoding is stipulated as Encoding.Unknown, indicating that it should be discovered instead. Alternatives include a set of both *explicit* and *implicit* encodings, where the former describe exactly the format of contained text, and the latter indicate that file inspection is required. For example, Encoding.UTF8N, Encoding.UTF16LE, and Encoding.UTF32BE are explicit encodings; Encoding.Unknown and Encoding.UTF16 are of the implicit variety.

---

Note ➡ When writing to a UnicodeFile, the encoding must, at that time, be known in order to transform the output appropriately (injecting a BOM header is optional when writing). When reading, the encoding may be declared as known or unknown.

---

The read method returns the current content of the file. The write method sets the file content and file length to the provided array. The append method adds content to the tail of the file. When appending, it is your responsibility to ensure the existing and current encodings are correctly matched. Methods to inspect and manipulate the underlying file hierarchy and to check the status of a file or folder are made available via the path attribute in a manner similar to File.

UnicodeFile will relay exceptions when an underlying operating system or file system error occurs, or when an error occurs while content is being decoded.


## Using Additional FileSystem Controls

FileSystem is where various file system controls are exposed. At this time, tango.io.FileSystem provides facilities for retrieving and setting the current working directory, and for converting a path into its absolute form. To retrieve the current directory name, do this:

```
auto name = FileSystem.getDirectory;
```

Changing the current directory is similar in operation:

```
FileSystem.setDirectory (name);
```

FileSystem.toAbsolute accepts a FilePath instance and converts it into absolute form relevant to the current working directory. Absolute form generally begins with a path separator, or a storage device identifier, and contains no instances of a dot (.) or double dot (..) anywhere in the path. If the provided path is already absolute, it is returned untouched.

Failing to set or retrieve the current directory will cause an exception to be thrown. Passing an invalid path to FileSystem.toAbsolute will also result in an exception being thrown.

## Working with FileRoots

The storage devices of the file system are exposed via the FileRoots module. On Win32, roots represent drive letters; on Linux, they represent devices located via /etc/mtab. To list the file storage devices available, try this:

```
import tango.io.Console,
       tango.io.FileRoots;

foreach (name; FileRoots.list)
        Cout (name).newline;
```

An IOException will be thrown where an underlying operating system or file system error occurs.

## Listing Files and Folders Using FileScan

The FileScan module wraps the file traversal functionality from FilePath in order to provide something more concrete. The principal distinction is that FileScan visits each discovered folder and generates a list of both the files and the folders that contain those files.

To generate a list of D files and the folders where they reside, you might try this:

```
import tango.io.Stdout,
       tango.io.FileScan;

char[] root = ".";
Stdout.formatln ("Scanning '{}'", root);
auto scan = (new FileScan)(root, ".d");

Stdout.format ("\n{} Folders\n", scan.folders.length);
foreach (folder; scan.folders)
        Stdout.format ("{}\n", folder);

Stdout.format ("\n{0} Files\n", scan.files.length);
```

```
foreach (file; scan.files)
        Stdout.format ("{}\n", file);

Stdout.formatln ("\n{} Errors", scan.errors.length);
foreach (error; scan.errors)
        Stdout (error).newline;
```

The example executes a sweep across all files ending with .d, beginning at the current folder and extending across all subfolders. Each folder that contains at least one located file is displayed on the console, followed by a list of the located files themselves. The output would look something like this abbreviated listing:

```
Scanning '\d\import\tango\io'

8 Folders
\d\import\tango\io\compress
\d\import\tango\io\stream
\d\import\tango\io\vfs
. . .
\d\import\tango\io

40 Files
\d\import\tango\io\Buffer.d
\d\import\tango\io\compress\BzipStream.d
\d\import\tango\io\compress\ZlibStream.d
\d\import\tango\io\Console.d
\d\import\tango\io\File.d
\d\import\tango\io\FileConduit.d
\d\import\tango\io\Stdout.d
. . .
\d\import\tango\io\stream\DataFileStream.d
\d\import\tango\io\stream\DataStream.d
\d\import\tango\io\stream\FileStream.d
\d\import\tango\io\stream\FormatStream.d
\d\import\tango\io\stream\LineStream.d
\d\import\tango\io\stream\TextFileStream.d
\d\import\tango\io\stream\TypedStream.d
\d\import\tango\io\stream\UtfStream.d
0 Errors
```

For more sophisticated file filtering, FileScan may be customized via a delegate:

```
bool delegate (FilePath path, bool folder)
```

The return value of the delegate should be true to add the instance, or false to ignore it. The parameter folder indicates whether the instance is a directory or a file.

FileScan throws no explicit exceptions, but those from FilePath.toList will be gathered up and exposed to the user via scan.errors instead. These are generally file system failures reported by the underlying operating system.

## Manipulating Paths Using FilePath

In the Tango library, file and folder locations are typically described by a FilePath instance. In some cases, a method accepting a textual file name will wrap it with a FilePath before continuing.

A number of common file and folder operations are exposed via FilePath—including creation, renaming, removal, and the generation of folder content lists—along with a handful of attributes such as file size and various timestamps. You can check to see if a path exists, whether it is write-protected, and whether it represents a file or a folder.

Creating a FilePath is straightforward: you provide the constructor with a char[]. File paths containing non-ASCII characters should be UTF-8 encoded:

```
import tango.io.FilePath;

auto path = new FilePath ("/dev/tango/io/FilePath.d");
```

With a FilePath instance in hand, each component can be efficiently inspected and adjusted. You can retrieve or replace each individual component of the path, such as the file name, the extension, the folder segment, the root, and so on. FilePath can be considered to be a specialized string editor, with hooks into the file system. Using the previous example, Table 7-4 highlights each component.

*Table 7-4. Inspecting FilePath Components*

| Component | Content |
| --- | --- |
| Cout (path); | /dev/tango/io/FilePath.d |
| Cout (path.folder); | /dev/tango/io/ |
| Cout (path.file); | FilePath.d |
| Cout (path.name); | FilePath |
| Cout (path.suffix); | .d |
| Cout (path.ext); | d |

Changing component values is straightforward, too, as Table 7-5 illustrates. In the table, we are both adjusting a component and showing the resultant change to the path itself.

*Table 7-5. Adjusting FilePath Components*

| Component | Content |
| --- | --- |
| Cout (path.set("tango/io/Console.d")); | tango/io/Console.d |
| Cout (path.folder("other")); | other/Console.d |
| Cout (path.file("myfile.x.y")); | other/myfile.x.y |
| Cout (path.name("test")); | other/test.x.y |
| Cout (path.suffix("txt")); | other/test.txt |

You can also append and prepend text to a FilePath, and appropriate separators will be inserted where required. Another useful tool is the pop function, which removes the rightmost text (in place) such that a parent folder segment is exposed. Successive use of pop will result in a root folder, or just a simple name. Another handy one is dup, which can be used to make a copy of another FilePath, like so:

```
import tango.io.FilePath;

auto path = FilePath ("/dev/tango/io/FilePath.d");
auto other = path.dup.name ("other");
```

The original path is left intact, while other has the same components except for a different name.

When you are creating "physical" files and folders, a distinction is required between the two. Use path.createFile to create a new file and path.createFolder to create a new folder. The full path to a folder can be constructed using path.create, which checks for the existence of each folder in the hierarchy and creates it where not present.

---

Note ➡ An exception will be raised if path.create encounters an existing file with the same name as a provided path segment.

---

Renaming a file can also move it from one place to another:

```
path.rename ("/directory/otherfilename");
```

Copying a file retains the original timestamps:

```
path.copy ("source");
```

You can remove a file or a folder like this:

```
path.remove;
```

List the content of a folder like this:

```
import tango.io.Console,
       tango.io.FilePath;

foreach (name; path.toList)
         Cout (name).newline;
```

You can customize the generated results by passing toList a filter delegate with the same signature noted in the previous section. Returning false from the filter causes a specific path to be ignored. An additional, lower-level foreach iterator exposes further detail:

```
import tango.io.Stdout,
       tango.io.FilePath;

foreach (info; path)
         Stdout.formatln("path {}, name {}, size {}, is folder {}",
                   info.path, info.name, info.size, info.folder);
```

When using FilePath, any errors produced by the underlying file system will cause an IOException to be raised. For example, attempting to remove a nonexistent or read-only file will generate an exception.

---

Tip ➡ FilePath assumes both path and name are present within the provided file path, and therefore may split what is otherwise a logically valid path. Specifically, the name attribute of a FilePath is considered to be the segment following a rightmost path separator, and thus a folder identifier can become mapped to the name property instead of explicitly remaining with the path property. This follows the intent of treating file and folder paths in an identical manner: as a name with an optional ancestral structure. When you do not want this assumption about the path and name to be made, it is possible (and legitimate) to bias the interpretation by adding a trailing path separator. Doing so will result in an empty name attribute and a longer path attribute.

---

This concludes our look at some of the I/O facilities in Tango, and yet we've barely scratched the surface! Tango I/O offers various network-oriented packages to support HTTP and FTP protocols, for example. It also hosts a digest-message package, nonblocking I/O support, a data-compression package, and more.

In the next (and last) chapter, you'll find a general overview of additional packages within the Tango library.

# CHAPTER 8

# The Other Packages

Here we are at the last chapter. You've been introduced to a great deal about D and have learned about some of Tango's packages. In this chapter, we'll give you a whirlwind tour of the remaining packages.

First, we'll look at each package from a high level, so you can get a basic overview of the functionality it provides. Then we'll highlight some of the most interesting bits with more detail. Our goal is to give you an idea of what Tango is capable of and where to look in the documentation for more information.

## The Package Rundown

When reading the following package overviews, you'll notice that most of the functionality is commonly found in the standard libraries of other languages. If you look at the source or the documentation, you'll find that some of the interfaces are familiar. The developers of Tango reinvented wheels only when they thought it necessary. When they didn't, they took advantage of successful designs from other languages. The result is that programmers migrating to D will often feel at home with Tango. You may also find a pleasant surprise or two.

### tango.core

The `tango.core` package is the heart of Tango. It contains the public interface to the Tango runtime, the garbage collector interface, data structures and functions for runtime type identification, all exceptions thrown by the library, array manipulation routines, a thread module, routines for performing atomic operations, and more.

In the subpackage `tango.core.sync`, you'll find several modules that are useful for concurrent programming. Those who have experience working with multiple threads will recognize the purpose of these modules based on their names: `Barrier`, `Condition`, `Mutex`, `ReadWriteMutex`, and `Semaphore`. If you need to deal with any major synchronization issues in your Tango applications, `tango.core.sync` is the place to look for a solution.

## tango.math

The `tango.math` package contains a handful of modules that provide a variety of mathematical operations. Some of them are similar, or identical, to the operations available in the C standard library. Tango also exposes the C math routines directly in the `tango.stdc.math` module, but you are encouraged to use `tango.math.Math` in its stead. Where possible, the Tango versions of the functions are optimized. They also take advantage of platform-specific extensions. Furthermore, `tango.math.Math` includes some functions not found in the standard C math library.

   In addition to the usual suspects, some advanced mathematical special functions are found in `tango.math.Bessel`, `tango.math.ErrorFunction`, and `tango.math.GammaFunction`. For statistics applications, a set of cumulative probability distribution functions live in `tango.math.Probability`. More down to earth, several low-level, floating-point functions are included in `tango.math.IEEE`. Finally, `tango.math.Random` defines a class that you can use to generate random numbers.

## tango.stdc

The `tango.stdc` package is your interface to the C world. If it's in the C standard library, you'll find it in `tango.stdc`. Keep in mind, though, that most of the functionality here is available elsewhere in Tango.

   When creating D applications from the ground up, it is recommended that you use the higher-level Tango APIs if possible. However, the `tango.stdc` package is very useful for quickly porting applications to D from C or C++. POSIX programmers may also find a need, from time to time, to drop down into low-level POSIX routines. They will find the `tango.stdc.posix` package very helpful.

   One module that you'll find yourself using often when interfacing with C code is `tango.stdc.stringz`. This module provides utility functions to convert between C-style and D-style strings. Because most D strings are not `null`-terminated, they need to be modified by adding a `null` terminator before passing them to any C library routine. Failure to do so can result in undefined behavior (but usually you get a segmentation fault). The following two functions will be most useful to you:

```
char* toStringz (char[] s)
char[] fromUtf8z (char* s)
```

   Use `toStringz` to convert D strings to `null`-terminated C strings, and `fromUtf8z` for the reverse operation. `Utf16` versions of the functions operate on `wchar` strings.

Note ➡ You'll notice that the module names in the `tango.stdc` package are all lowercase, whereas other modules names in Tango are uppercase. This is done to easily distinguish between modules that bind to C libraries and those that are pure D.

## tango.sys

The `tango.sys` package exposes functions from the operating system API. It contains three subpackages: `sys.darwin`, `sys.linux`, and `sys.win32`. The first two, for Mac and Linux platforms, respectively, primarily contain modules that publicly import all of the POSIX modules from `tango.stdc.posix`. These can be accessed directly via `tango.sys.darwin.darwin` and `tango.sys.linux.linux`. You won't find a `tango.sys.win32.win32` module. Instead, there is `tango.sys.win32.UserGdi`. However, it's usually better just to import `tango.sys.Common`, which publicly imports the appropriate module based on the current platform at compile time.

You'll also find other useful modules in this package. `tango.sys.Environment` exposes system environment settings. `tango.sys.Pipe` and `tango.sys.Process` together allow you to work with piped processes in a system-agnostic way.

## tango.util

The `tango.util` package contains useful tools that don't squarely fit in any of the other packages. At the top level, you'll find `tango.util.ArgParser` and `tango.util.PathUtil`. The former provides an easy means of parsing command-line arguments. The latter is a set of routines useful for manipulating file path strings.

In `tango.util.collection`, you'll find a handy set of collection classes. We'll briefly examine this package in the "Collections" section later in the chapter. `tango.util.log` contains an extensible logging API that can be configured and reconfigured at runtime. We'll take a closer look at this package in the "Logging" section later in this chapter.

# Threads and Fibers

Most modern programming languages have some support for concurrent programming built in to the language, available in a library, or both. D is no exception. This is especially important now that multicore processors have become mainstream. Where concurrent programming issues were once primarily the realm of server developers, these days, they are becoming more of a concern for desktop application developers as well. D sports a few features to assist with concurrent programming, and Tango builds on that foundation with several modules that will ease the task. In this section, we'll take a peek at two of them.

## Threads

By far, the module you'll use most often when creating multithreaded applications with D and Tango is tango.core.Thread. In this module, you'll find a class that allows you to easily create and start multiple kernel threads in a platform-independent manner. Here is a simple example of one way to use the Thread class:

```
import tango.io.Stdout;
import tango.core.Thread;


void main()
{
```

```
    void printDg()
    {
        Thread thisThread = Thread.getThis;

        for(int i=0; i<10; ++i)
        {
            Stdout.formatln("{}: {}", thisThread.name, i);

        }

                Stdout.formatln("{} is going to sleep!", thisThread.name);
        Thread.sleep(1.0);        // Sleep for 1 second
        Stdout.formatln("{} is awake.", Thread.name);
    }

    Thread thread1 = new Thread(&printDg);
    thread1.name = "Thread #1";
```

```
Thread thread2 = new Thread(&printDg);
thread2.name = "Thread #2";

thread1.start();
thread2.start();

thread_joinAll();
Stdout("Both threads have exited").newline;
}
```

In this example, two threads are created and given a delegate in the constructor. The Thread class has two constructors: one that takes a delegate and one that takes a function pointer. This allows you to use free functions, class methods, inner functions, or anonymous delegates as the thread's worker function. Remember that pointers to class methods and inner functions are treated as delegates, whereas pointers to free functions are not.

The example also demonstrates a handful of thread API calls. First, in the printDg function, you'll notice the call to Thread.getThis. This is a static method that returns a reference to the currently executing thread. printDg uses the returned reference in order to access its name property when printing out messages. It calls Thread.sleep with an argument of 1.0, which puts the thread to sleep for 1 second. There is also a static yield method, which can be used to surrender the remainder of the current time slice.

Notice the call to the free function thread_joinAll near the end of the listing. The Thread class has a method, join, which can be used to wait for a specific thread to finish execution. For example, we could have called thread2.join() to wait until just thread2 completed. Instead, we chose to call thread_joinAll. This blocks the thread in which it was called while it waits for all currently active, non-daemon threads to complete. It also shows that there is more to the tango.core.Thread module than just the Thread class. It includes several free functions, all prefixed thread_, which allow you to manipulate all active threads at once.

---

Note ➡ A *daemon thread* is one that is intended to be used to perform a task for another thread. For example, a thread that runs in the background to load a resource could be considered a daemon thread. A thread can be flagged as a daemon by setting its isDaemon property to true.

---

The next example performs the same task as the previous one, but does so by extending the Thread class with a specific subclass. Notice that the run method of the subclass is passed as a delegate to the superclass constructor.

```
import tango.io.Stdout;
import tango.core.Thread;

class MyThread : Thread
{
    int id;

    this(int id)
    {
        super(&run);
        this.id = id;
    }

    void run()
    {
        for(int i=0; i<10; ++i)
        {
            Stdout.formatln("Thread {}: {}", id, i);
        }

        Stdout.formatln("Thread #{} is going to sleep!", id);
        Thread.sleep(1.0);        // Sleep for 1 second
        Stdout.formatln("Thread #{} has awakened and will now exit.", id);
    }
}

void main()
{
    Thread thread1 = new MyThread(1);
    Thread thread2 = new MyThread(2);

    thread1.start();
    thread2.start();

    thread_joinAll();
    Stdout("Both threads have exited").newline;
}
```

# Fibers

Whereas the Thread class is used to create kernel threads, the Fiber class, also found in tango.core.Thread, is used to create what are sometimes called *user threads*, or in some scripting languages, *coroutines*. Conceptually, threads execute within a process, and fibers execute within a thread.

Perhaps the most important difference between a fiber and a thread is that the user can stop execution of a fiber for a period of time and later resume execution at the point where it was stopped. In other words, you have complete control over the execution of a fiber (assuming, of course, that you programmed the logic for the fiber yourself!). The following shows a simple example of using a fiber:

```
import tango.io.Stdout;
import tango.core.Thread;

void main()
{
    void printDg()
    {
        for(int i=0; i<10; ++i)
        {
            Stdout.formatln("i = {}", i);
            Stdout("Yielding fiber.").newline;
            Fiber.yield();
            Stdout("Back in the fiber").newline;
        }
    }

    Fiber f = new Fiber(&printDg);
    for(int i=0; i<10; ++i)
    {
        Stdout("Calling fiber.").newline;
        f.call();
    }
}
```

The call method of the Fiber class causes the delegate, or function pointer, passed to the fiber to execute. To yield control back to the call site, the static Fiber.yield method can be called at any time from within the delegate. When call is next called on the same fiber object, execution will resume immediately after the last yield.

Bell, et al.

Fibers do not need to be executed by a single thread. You can pass a fiber instance from one thread to another, no matter its current state. For example, you could use a handful of threads to continually execute dozens of fibers, instead of creating dozens of threads. At any time, you can check a `Fiber`'s `state` property to determine its current status: `Fiber.EXEC` means it is currently executing, `Fiber.HOLD` means it has yielded, and `Fiber.TERM` indicates that execution has completed.

# Collections

Collections, or data structures, are an essential part of a solid standard library in modern programming languages. Many programmers find that D's dynamic and associative arrays provide enough functionality out of the box, so they don't need separate collection classes for some tasks. However, there is certainly a need for solid, templated collection classes that go beyond what the built-in arrays can do. The `tango.util.collection` package fills that need.

Rather than starting from scratch and creating an entirely new collection interface from the ground up, the Tango developers based their design on an existing API: Doug Lea's `collections` package for Java. In `tango.util.collection`, you'll find a set of collection classes that are useful in a variety of situations. They are based on four basic constructs: *bags*, *sets*, *sequences*, and *maps*. All collections implement the `tango.util.collection.model.Collection` interface. They also implement more interfaces depending on the type of collection and the operations supported.

## Bags

Bags are collections that allow multiple occurrences of any given element; that is, you can add the same element to a bag more than once. A bag may or may not be ordered. Any collection that wants to call itself a bag should implement the `tango.util.collection.model.Bag` interface. Alternatively, a collection can subclass the abstract `tango.util.collection.impl.BagCollection` class, which implements the necessary interfaces and provides some default behavior.

Currently, the `tango.util.collection` package includes two `Bag` implementations:

- `TreeBag` is a red-black tree implementation. This is useful when you need to quickly search for a particular element, but don't care about the order of the elements.

- ArrayBag is an unordered collection of elements stored in one or more internal buffers. This is useful when you need to frequently iterate the elements, don't care about the order, and don't need to find a specific element.

---

Note ➡ A *red-black tree* is a data structure that is often used to store data that needs to be searched efficiently. For more information, see http://en.wikipedia.org/wiki/Red_black_tree.

---

The following example demonstrates a common use of array bags:

```
import tango.io.Stdout;
import tango.util.collection.ArrayBag;

class MyClass
{
    void print()
    {
        Stdout("Hello ArrayBag").newline;
    }
}

void main()
{
    // Fill an array bag with 10 instances of MyClass
    ArrayBag!(MyClass) bag = new ArrayBag!(MyClass);
    for(int i=0; i<10; ++i)
        bag.add(new MyClass);

    // Iterate the bag and perform a common operation
    foreach(mc; bag)
        mc.print();
}
```

This example shows a typical use case for Bag. We don't care in what order the instances of MyClass are stored in the collection. All we care about is that we can iterate it and perform a common operation. Here, we do only one iteration. But in a real application, you would likely need to do so more than one. Obviously, you could achieve the same result with a dynamic array. One of the advantages of using an ArrayBag rather than an array is that you can easily remove or insert elements with a single function call. Another is that if you stick to using methods in the Bag and Collection interfaces, you can easily change the implementation to another bag type later if necessary.

Bell, et al.

## Sets

Sets are similar to bags, with the important distinction that they don't allow duplicates. All sets implement the tango.util.collection.model.set interface. As a shortcut, new implementations can subclass the abstract tango.util.collection.impl.SetCollection class.

The collection package currently contains only one Set implementation: HashSet. This is an implementation backed by a hash table. Each element you add is both a value and a key in the table. This collection is useful when every element needs to be unique, and you don't need to add or remove elements frequently. Use the contains method to determine if an element exists in the set. If you want to provide a custom hash algorithm for your own data types, you should override Object.toHash in your classes and add a toHash method to your structs. Both methods should return a type of hash_t.

Here is a code snippet that demonstrates a common use of hash sets:

```
import tango.io.Stdout;
import tango.util.collection.HashSet;

// Given a number n, generates the next number in the
// Fibonacci sequence
int fibonacci(int n)
{
    if(n == 0) return 0;
    else if(n == 1) return 1;
    else return fibonacci(n-1) + fibonacci(n-2);
}

void main()
{
    // Create a hash set to store integers
    HashSet!(int) set = new HashSet!(int);

    // Populate the set with the first 10 numbers in the Fibonacci sequence
    for(int i=0; i<10; ++i)
        set.add(fibonacci(i));

    // Print the sequence to the console
    foreach(i; set)
        Stdout(i).newline;

    // Now test the numbers 0 - 19 to see if they are in the set.
    // Print PASS if a number is in the set, and FAIL if it isn't.
```

```
for(int i=0; i<20; ++i)
{
    if(set.contains(i))
        Stdout.formatln("{}: PASS", i);
    else
        Stdout.formatln("{}: FAIL", i);
}
}
```

This example shows a common use case of hash sets, but also highlights a couple of "gotchas." The set is populated with a unique group of elements—in this case, the first ten numbers of the Fibonacci sequence. Then another group of elements is tested one at a time against the set. If the set contains the element, one action is taken. If not, a different action is taken. Quite often, a failed `contains` test will indicate failure of some sort.

Astute readers may be scratching their heads, wondering what we meant when we said "a unique group of elements" in relation to the Fibonacci sequence. The first ten numbers of the Fibonacci sequence are 0, 1, 1, 2, 3, 5, 8, 13, 21, 34. As you can see, the numbers in the set are not all unique, since the number 1 appears twice. If you run the program, you'll notice that the `foreach` loop that prints out each element of the set prints only a single 1. The set actually contains nine elements, rather than the ten we added. Remember that *sets do not allow duplicates.*

Another gotcha this code demonstrates is clearly visible if you compile and execute it. The `foreach` loop that prints the elements in the set outputs the following on one machine:

```
0
1
2
34
3
5
8
13
21
```

Everything looks nice and neat except for that big, ugly 34 stuck in the middle. Sets make no guarantees about the order in which elements are stored. So not only can you not store both 1s from the Fibonacci sequence in a set, you can't even print the sequence in order. That goes to show that sets are a poor choice to store the Fibonacci sequence! However, sets are perfect for elements that meet the criteria. For example, you might use a set to store a fixed range of IP addresses, where each address needs to be unique.

# Sequences

Bags and sets are chaos incarnate. When it's order you need, sequences are here to save the day. Sequences are guaranteed to store elements in the order in which you add them (unless, of course, you decide to sort the collection based on some other criteria). Sequences may also allow duplicates, though that depends on the implementation. Because sequences are ordered, they provide order-oriented operations for adding elements, rather than just a simple add method. You can append, prepend, and insert elements.

All sequence implementations should implement the `tango.util.collection.model.Seq` interface. The `tango.util.collection.impl.SeqCollection` abstract class is a good starting point for new implementations. The `collection` package contains three sequence implementations:

- `LinkSeq` is a linked-list implementation of the `Seq` interface. These collections have a constant cost for adding, removing, and inserting elements. They can be iterated at a constant cost as well, but finding a particular element in the list can be expensive.

- `CircularSeq` has the same general characteristics as `LinkSeq`, but is doubly linked with a head and a tail. This makes a big difference when you need to work with a sequence in reverse. Accessing the tail of a `LinkSeq` is a $O(n)$ operation, where $n$ is the number of elements in the list. Accessing the tail of a `CircularSeq` is a $O(1)$ operation.

- `ArraySeq`, in addition to implementing the `Seq` interface, provides a set of methods that allow you to set a specific capacity. When the capacity is reached, the internal array is dynamically resized to accommodate more elements. You can adjust the capacity or resize the sequence at any time. Note that when you first allocate an `ArraySeq`, no memory is allocated internally for the array. When you add the first element, the array is allocated using the default capacity. Since adding or inserting an element can cause the internal array to be resized, it can be an expensive operation.

When you know you need a sequence, choosing between the array implementation and one of the linked-list implementations can sometimes be a tough decision. In general, if you will be frequently inserting, appending, or prepending elements, you're probably better off with one of the LinkedList implementations in order to avoid potentially expensive resizing. If you need to access individual elements frequently from the middle of the sequence, you're better off with an ArraySeq. The difficulty comes when you need to frequently add elements to the collection *and* access them individually. When the choice is not obvious, the best thing to do is test, test, profile, and test and profile some more.

In the following example, we revisit our Fibonacci example using an ArraySeq, which is much better suited to the purpose than the HashSet we used previously.

```
import tango.io.Stdout;
import tango.util.collection.ArraySeq;

// Given a number n, generates the next number in the
// Fibonacci sequence
int fibonacci(int n)
{
    if(n == 0) return 0;
    else if(n == 1) return 1;
    else return fibonacci(n-1) + fibonacci(n-2);
}

void main()
{
    // Create an array sequence to store integers
    ArraySeq!(int) seq = new ArraySeq!(int);

    // We are using a fixed set of numbers, so set the capacity to 10
    seq.capacity = 10;

    // Populate the collection
    for(int i=0; i<10; ++i)
        seq.append(fibonacci(i));

    // Print the sequence to the console
    foreach(i; seq)
        Stdout(i).newline;

    // Now test the numbers 0-19 to see if they are in the collection
    // Print PASS if a number is in the collection, and FAIL if it isn't.
    for(int i=0; i<20; ++i)
    {
```

```
        if(seq.contains(i))
            Stdout.formatln("{}: PASS", i);
        else
            Stdout.formatln("{}: FAIL", i);
    }
}
```

The code here is very similar to that used previously with the hash set. The biggest difference is that we call the append method to add each number to the end of the sequence. This means that when we iterate the sequence, each number will be returned in the order it was added. If you compile and execute the program, you should see the following output from the foreach loop that prints each element in the collection:

```
0
1
1
2
3
5
8
13
21
34
```

This output is much more suitable for the Fibonacci sequence. The collection contains both of the 1s and, on iteration, returns each number in the proper sequence. They're not called *sequences* for nothing!

# Maps

Maps are useful things. They allow you to take an element of one type and associate it with an element of another type as a key/value pair. D's built-in associative arrays are maps. Tango maps have the same functionality, but go beyond the simple built-in operations. All maps should implement the tango.util.collection.model.Map interface or extend the tango.util.collection.impl.MapCollection abstract class.

Tango ships with three map implementations: LinkMap, TreeMap, and HashMap. The difference between the three implementations is largely based on the time it takes to complete the operations from the Map interface. Many of the operations of LinkMap are $O(n)$, whereas HashMap operations typically have a best-case performance of $O(1)$ and worst-case performance of O(*n*). Several of the TreeMap operations tend to be somewhere in the middle, at O(log *n*). It's not immediately obvious which implementation to choose without looking at the performance characteristics of each operation. Fortunately, the performance of each operation is documented well. A quick overview can give you a general idea of which implementation is more suitable for certain situations.

When you just need somewhere to store key/value pairs for iteration and don't need to perform any lookups by key, a LinkMap is a perfect choice. Doing key lookups on one of these can be really expensive if there are a lot of elements. If you are frequently looking up values by their keys, but not doing much iteration of all elements, you'll be better off with a HashMap. The TreeMap is perhaps best used when you have a large number of key/value pairs to add. When a HashMap contains a large number of elements, collisions are more likely, making each bucket more likely to reach the worst-case performance during a lookup. TreeMaps have a predictable lookup time for both keys and values, and you don't suffer as much for adding more elements. Ultimately, though, it's the profiler that should tell you which implementation is best suited to your situation. This is true for all of the collections, really, but more so for the maps.

## More on Collections

In addition to the collections themselves, the tango.util.collection package contains a few other useful items that can make your use of collections more robust. You'll find different types of iterators, such as an IterleavingIterator and a FilteringIterator, which can be used in place of the foreach loop. A Comparator can be used to sort elements in a collection. You can even use a special delegate, called a *screener*, to allow only elements that meet certain criteria to be added to a collection.

The collection package can do quite a lot for you, so that you don't need to roll your own. You can get by with D's built-in dynamic and associative arrays for many simple tasks, but for more complex uses, you'll need to manually implement some of what the collection package already does for you. Remember that when you find yourself adding more and more code to manage your dynamic array-based set!

# Logging

Tango's logging API, which is defined by the modules in the tango.util.log package, is a flexible and extensible framework that can be configured at runtime. Like the collection API, the logging API is not something the Tango developers created out of thin air. One of the most popular logging APIs in existence is a Java library called Log4J. The design of Tango's logging framework closely follows that of Log4J, so if you are coming from a Java background, you may already be familiar with it.

In order to use the log package, you need to know two basic things: how to create a Logger and what log levels are.

# Loggers

The following code demonstrates how to create a Logger instance and log a simple message.

```
import tango.util.log.Configurator;
import tango.util.log.Log;

void main()
{
    Logger logger = Log.getLogger("MyLogger");
    logger.info("Hello world");
}
```

This example imports the tango.util.log.Configurator module. This module contains a static constructor that configures the logging system to send all output to the system console. It sends output through Stderr by default.

The call to Log.getLogger creates a new logger instance and assigns it the name "MyLogger". Names are important in the logging framework because, internally, the loggers are stored in a hierarchy based on their names. When a new logger is added to the hierarchy, it receives the settings and properties of its parent logger. If we were to create another logger, with a call such as Log.getLogger("MyLogger.Child"), the "." in the name would indicate that the new logger is a child of the instance named "MyLogger". For this reason, it is common to create loggers named after the module in which they reside.

The "MyLogger" instance is also a child. Even though we did not explicitly assign a parent to it, it was added to the hierarchy as a child of the special root logger. The root logger is created automatically by the framework. When the static constructor in the Configurator module runs, it is the root logger that is being configured. When a new logger instance is created as a child of the root, it receives the same configuration. If you need to explicitly access the root logger, you can do so via the static method Log.getRootLogger.

# Log Levels

It's very handy to be able to configure different "degrees" of logging output. For example, some output is useful for debugging but isn't really a good idea to leave in the final release. Traditionally, C and C++ developers would compile *debug* and *release* versions of their software, with debug logging enabled in the former and disabled in the latter. This works some of the time, but experience has shown that it can be very useful to enable debug logging in the release version as well. The solution is to allow debug logging to be configurable at runtime rather than at compile time.

Log levels allow you to specify different degrees of log output. You can set six different log levels:

- Trace is intended to be used for debug output.

- Info is intended for logging informational messages, such as those that mark the flow of an application.

- Warn is intended for logging warning messages, such as in response to events that aren't really errors but are unexpected or unusual behavior.

- Error is intended for logging errors from which the program can recover.

- Fatal is intended for logging errors that cause the program to exit.

- None turns off the logger entirely.

The levels are listed here from lowest priority to highest. When a level is set on a logger instance, all messages that are intended for that level and higher will be logged, while messages intended for lower levels will be ignored. For example, setting the Trace level turns on logging for all levels, while setting the Error level restricts logging to just Error and Fatal level messages. Although you can assign any meaning you want to each level, it is recommended that you follow the suggested intent, as noted in the list.

You can associate log output with a particular level in two ways. The Logger class has an append method, which accepts two parameters: a log level and a message string. Most of the time, though, you'll want to use one of the five shortcut methods, which each accept a single string as a parameter: trace, info, warn, error, or fatal. The following example shows how to set the level of a logger and use each of the logging methods:

```
import tango.util.log.Configurator;
import tango.util.log.Log;

void main()
```

```
{
    Logger logger = Log.getLogger("MyLogger");

    // Turn off Trace messages
    logger.level = Logger.Level.Info;

    logger.trace("I'm a trace message, but you can't see me!");
    logger.info("I'm an info message!");
    logger.warn("I'm a warn message!");
    logger.error("I'm an error message!");
    logger.fatal("I'm a fatal message!");
    logger.append(Logger.Level.Fatal, "I'm a fatal message, too!");

    // Turn Trace messages back on
    logger.level = Logger.level.Trace;

    logger.trace("Hey, you can see trace messages now!");
}
```

## More on Logging

What we've shown you so far is all you really need to know to use Tango's logging framework. But logging to the system console isn't always useful, particularly for applications that the end user runs in a window. It's much better to send log output to a file, and that's a simple thing to do. Tango lets you configure the target of log output with a construct called an *appender*.

Tango ships with six appender implementations:

- ConsoleAppender sends output to the system console and is configured by default when you import the Configurator module.

- FileAppender directs output to a file.

- RollingFileAppender directs output to one of a group of files based on a maximum size.

- SocketAppender sends output to a network socket and is useful for remote debugging.

- MailAppender e-mails log output somewhere.

- NullAppender sends log output nowhere and may be useful for benchmarking.

Of course, if none of the stock appenders meet your requirements, you can implement your own.

---

Note ➡ It's possible to have more than one appender attached to a logger via the addAppender method. In fact, newly created logs inherit the appenders of their parents, so any new appenders you add to a logger will cause output to be sent to it in addition to those inherited from the parent, unless you explicitly disable one or more of them.

---

You can also control the format of the log output by using a Layout implementation. Tango currently has a few implementations, all of which extend the base EventLayout class. The default configuration set up by the Configurator module uses the SimpleTimerLayout, which prepends to the output the number of milliseconds since the application started, the level of the message, and the name of the logger that wrote the message. The other stock layouts are all variations on this theme.

The following example shows how to create a logger that sends its output to a file using the SimpleTimerLayout:

```
import tango.util.log.Log;
import tango.util.log.FileAppender;
import tango.util.log.EventLayout;
import tango.io.FilePath;

void main()
{
    auto fa = new FileAppender(new FilePath("log.txt"), new SimpleTimerLayout);
    Log.getRootLogger.addAppender(fa);

    Logger logger = Log.getLogger("MyLogger");
    logger.info("Hello file appender!");
}
```

This should be enough to get you going with the logging framework right away. Notice that the Configurator is not imported, since we are configuring the root logger ourselves. As an exercise, go ahead and add an import statement for tango.util.log.Configurator, and see what happens when you run it.

# And That's Not All!

Tango has more than we've covered so far and more that may be added to the library in the future. At the time of this writing, two very recent additions to Tango are the `tango.io.vfs` and `tango.net.cluster` packages.

The `tango.io.vfs` package is a virtual file system (VFS) API. The goal of this package is to allow users to access disparate file systems through a uniform interface, regardless of the current platform. The basic premise is that you mount specific paths to the VFS, and then read and write resources wherever they may be. Mounted paths could be from the local file system, a remote file system, or a zip archive. The package is still in development, so not all of the features are implemented yet, and the design will likely fluctuate over the next few months. As you're reading this, it may or may not be in its final state.

The `tango.net.cluster` package is not the sort of API you will find in your average standard library. This ambitious package aims to aid you in creating software that can be clustered on multiple physical machines. Run on one machine or run on a dozen, add new machines or remove old ones, and your software will still do the right thing. If a machine in the cluster dies, the others will take over its workload. This is a highly specialized package that isn't going to be useful to everyone, but it will make a wide range of applications much more accessible to Tango users. It may be useful for enterprise application servers, massively multiplayer game servers, or distributed programs doing intensive number-crunching.

Finally, more packages are in the works. For example, in the summer of 2007, the Tango team announced a `tango.graphics` package. This package will, at a minimum, provide an API for rendering 2D graphics. It will be usable on the server side for generating images on the fly, or on the desktop for rendering to application windows. It will take advantage of hardware acceleration where it's available, and otherwise fall back to software rendering. There are still a lot of design and use-case details to be ironed out, but the package is expected to see a beta release in early 2008.

Printed in the United States
100981LV00004B/31-50/A